The Official Book of The Shih Tzu

JO ANN WHITE

including
**The Illustrated Guide to the Shih Tzu Standard
Endorsed by the American Shih Tzu Club, Inc.**

Illustrations by Gladys Ray.
COURTESY OF BETTY WINTERS.

Illustrated Guide ©1997, American Shih Tzu Club, Inc.
Computer imaging portion of Illustrated Guide © 1995, The American Kennel Club, Inc., courtesy AKC Judging Research and Development Department.

© by T.F.H. Publications, Inc.

Distributed in the UNITED STATES to the Pet Trade by T.F.H. Publications, Inc., One T.F.H. Plaza, Neptune City, NJ 07753; on the Internet at www.tfh.com; in CANADA Rolf C. Hagen Inc., 3225 Sartelon St. Laurent-Montreal Quebec H4R 1E8; Pet Trade by H & L Pet Supplies Inc., 27 Kingston Crescent, Kitchener, Ontario N2B 2T6; in ENGLAND by T.F.H. Publications, PO Box 15, Waterlooville PO7 6BQ; in AUSTRALIA AND THE SOUTH PACIFIC by T.F.H. (Australia), Pty. Ltd., Box 149, Brookvale 2100 N.S.W., Australia; in NEW ZEALAND by Brooklands Aquarium Ltd. 5 McGiven Drive, New Plymouth, RD1 New Zealand; in SOUTH AFRICA, Rolf C. Hagen S.A. (PTY.) LTD. P.O. Box 201199, Durban North 4016, South Africa; in Japan by T.F.H. Publications, Japan—Jiro Tsuda, 10-12-3 Ohjidai, Sakura, Chiba 285, Japan. Published by T.F.H. Publications, Inc.
MANUFACTURED IN THE
UNITED STATES OF AMERICA
BY T.F.H. PUBLICATIONS, INC.

Contents

About the Author

Jo Ann White accidentally found her first Shih Tzu in 1967 while looking for a Lhasa Apso for her parents and began showing him in Miscellaneous Class at the encouragement of his breeders. Thus began a love affair with this wonderful breed whose intensity has never waned. Showing and breeding on a limited scale ever since under her Heavenly Dynasty prefix, Jo Ann has bred and/or owned about 20 champions. In the 1970s and early 1980s, she handled Shih Tzu professionally and taught a breed-handling class. Although not an AKC licensed judge, she has judged puppy sweepstakes at Shih Tzu specialties across the country. Jo Ann also put an obedience title on her first champion Shih Tzu, who didn't want to stop going to dog shows when retired from the conformation ring and became the country's first dual-titled Shih Tzu bitch after only seven hours of classes. Jo Ann's not sure whether that says something about the breed's overall intelligence or whether it only happened because one very bright Shih Tzu was thrilled by an activity she didn't have to share with any of the other dogs, but it was a great experience! With her next Shih Tzu, she's hoping to try agility as well as conformation.

Shih Tzu breed columnist and features author for the *AKC Gazette* since 1988, Jo Ann served on the ASTC Board of Directors in the 1970s and again in the 1990s, and was ASTC President from 1995 to 1996. For many years, she has been an active member of the ASTC Education Committee, with a special interest in educating the new Shih Tzu owner. She is also a member of the club's Gene-Mapping Committee, which is involved in research to find a genetic marker for renal dysplasia in Shih Tzu.

Jo Ann now lives on the Gulf coast of Florida with her husband, a retired publishing executive, and two similarly retired (and very spoiled) Shih Tzu champions. A free-lance reference-book writer and editor specializing primarily in articles on Asia, Africa, Latin America, and Oceania for encyclopedias, she received a BA in History from Duke University and an MA in International Relations from New York University. In addition to this book and a pet-owner's guide to the Shih Tzu, she is author of *Impact! Asian Views of the West* and *African Views of the West.* She is also an avid cook and gardener.

Jo Ann has collected Foo dogs and other Oriental memorabilia for many years and speculates that her academic interest in Asia contributed to her initial fascination with an Asian breed of dog. The charm of the Shih Tzu themselves and the many friends in dogs she has made over the years did the rest!

Author Jo Ann White, showing one of her homebred champions. (Tatum)

Acknowledgments

My thanks to all of the ASTC members who cooperated in the writing of this book, and to the ASTC Board of Directors for the club's endorsement. Most especially, I would like to thank my successor as ASTC President, Sally Vilas, who reviewed the entire project; my husband Richard Lawall, who took all of the photographs for this book not otherwise credited and provided moral and organizational support; the many Shih Tzu fanciers who contributed their photographs; and the following individuals and organizations:

Ann Hickok Warner and Victor Joris, for their aid with information on the history of the breed and the club;

Richard Paquette, for his input on the Shih Tzu in Canada;

Wendy and Richard Paquette, Peter J. Rogers III, and Joe Walton, for their years of work on the Illustrated Guide to the Shih Tzu Standard;

Kandy Jones, for the text and illustrations for the section on haircuts for the pet Shih Tzu;

Peggy Hogg, for her review of the chapters dealing with showing in conformation, show grooming, and judging the Shih Tzu;

Bonnie Guggenheim and Joe Walton, for their help with the chapter on judging the Shih Tzu;

Cindy Smith, DVM, and Carlene Snyder, chair of the ASTC Health Committee, for reviewing the chapters on breeding and health;

Doris Pletl, Cindy Rhodes, Phyllis Celmer, Michael Shea-Zackin, and Sandy Crook of the U.S. Agility Training Center, for their help with the Shih Tzu in obedience, agility, and pet therapy;

Pat Martello and Carlene Snyder, for their contributions to the grooming and show training photo essays and text;

ASTC Bulletin editor Madonna Holko, for her encouragement and support throughout this project and her contributions to the material directed at the pet owner;

Betty Winters, for the donation of her late mother Gladys Ray's wonderful Shih Tzu sketches to the ASTC;

Dr. James Edwards and his staff in the AKC's Judging Research and Development Department, for the computer imaging section of the Illustrated Guide;

Delaware Valley Golden Retriever Rescue, for their input into the chapter on choosing a puppy;

Editor Andrew DePrisco and the T.F.H. staff that made this book so visually appealing;

T.F.H. Publications, Inc., for its generous contributions to the ASTC Gene-Mapping Funds;

and, especially, all of the many named and unnamed "old-timers" in our breed who have given of their time over the years to the ASTC, their local clubs, the Shih Tzu breed, and the sport of dogs. Without them and everything they have taught me, I could have never written this book. On behalf of all of them, may *The Official Book of the Shih Tzu* encourage newcomers to our breed to experience a lifetime of the rewards and friendships of the world of the Shih Tzu.

Jo Ann White

Gladys Ray

Introduction

A Shih Tzu is a big dog in a little package. Though small enough to live happily in a city apartment, it is sturdy and even-tempered, with few health problems. It loves people and other dogs of all shapes and sizes, and it is definitely not a watchdog. Many Shih Tzu almost never bark and would happily give a burglar a guided tour! This is an easy breed to spoil. Shih Tzu are very good at letting you know what they want, and if you're not careful you'll find that they train you instead of the other way around. If you want to romp, they're ready to go. If you want to rest, they'll curl up quietly next to you. We often joke that Shih Tzu are like potato chips–once you have one, you always want more!

All of these characteristics have made me a devoted Shih Tzu fan for more than 30 years. While a Shih Tzu is not the breed for everyone, because its long coat requires regular care and it is not an outside dog or a watchdog (or a sleeve dog), I think our breed justly deserves its popularity. I also think that every Shih Tzu breeder has a responsibility to see that the Shih Tzu continues to retain the qualities that make it such an ideal choice of breed for so many people, namely its wonderful temperament and good health.

I join with all of the members of the American Shih Tzu Club, Inc., in hoping that this book will help both the novice and the experienced fancier protect and preserve our wonderful breed.

Shih Tzu illustrations by Gladys Ray.
COURTESY OF BETTY WINTERS.

Early Development of the Shih Tzu

ogs of various sizes, shapes, and colors have been bred in China for centuries. Records substantiate the existence of short, square, "under the table" dogs from at least 1000 BC. By piecing together historical facts and documentary records, it is possible to some extent to follow the development in China of the breeding of dogs likely to be the ancestors of our present-day Shih Tzu.

The ancestry of the Shih Tzu is rather obscure, but it is probable that the breed is primarily of Tibetan origin. The history of the Tibetan "lion dogs" is interwoven with the tenets of Buddhism. The lion became closely associated with Buddhism in India, where the religion originated. But the lion was not indigenous to China, so the Chinese eunuchs and Tibetan monks bred their toy dogs to resemble the much larger beast. Ancient Chinese scrolls depict small dogs trimmed to look like lions, with ruffs around their necks and bracelets of hair around their ankles and tufts of hair at the tip of their clipped tails. Such lion dogs were also the subjects of Foo dog statuary, sometimes with harnesses and bridles, depicting them as the lion-steed of Buddha. The Buddhist bodhisattva (holy man) Manjusri, who is often depicted astride a Foo dog, was said to have had a pet dog that was often transformed into a lion. The entrance to a Buddhist temple is often guarded by a pair of Foo dogs, the male with its front foot on a ball; the female with its foot on a puppy (or puppies). Some owners still trim their cut-down Shih Tzu in lion-like clips much like those from ancient China.

The Shih Tzu (whose name in Chinese means "lion") is reputed to have been the oldest and smallest variety of the Tibetan "holy dogs" and bears some similarity to other Tibetan breeds such as the Lhasa Apso, the Tibetan Terrier, and the Tibetan Spaniel. Some breed historians argue that the flat faces and short noses of the Shih Tzu were more characteristic of other short-faced Oriental breeds such as the Pekingese, Pug, and Japanese Chin than of the ancient Tibetan breeds, whose longer muzzles were better adapted to the cold climate and high altitude of Tibet. Thus the Shih Tzu may have developed from the crossing of ancient Chinese and Tibetan breeds. In any case, the breeding of small, shaggy, lion-like dogs was a favorite pastime of succeeding imperial rulers for much of the long and illustrious history of China.

Prior to AD 624, documents show that small dogs were exported from Malta, Turkey, Greece, and Persia as gifts to the ruling Chinese emperors. It is likely that the first small Tibetan Lion Dogs from which the Shih Tzu is probably descended came to China during the Qing (Ch'ing) Dynasty (1644-62) as tributes from the Grand Lamas to the Chinese Imperial Court, and that the Chinese interbred these Tibetan dogs with the early Western imports and with the indigenous Pug and the Pekingese to create the distinctive "chrysanthemum-faced" Shih Tzu.

The existence of the Shih Tzu as we know it today is owed to the Dowager Empress Cixi (T'zu Hsi), whose kennel of Pugs, Pekingese, and Shih Tzu was world renowned. Although she carefully supervised the kennel during her lifetime and attempted to keep the three imperial breeds separate, the actual breeding was carried out by palace eunuchs who secretly crossed the breeds to reduce size and produce unusual and desirable markings. (Dogs were often bred to match the colors in the gowns of the court ladies.) An old Chinese description

Above and Below: Oriental "Foo dog" art depicts Shih Tzu and other ancient "lion dogs" that came to be considered sacred in Buddhism.

The contemporary Shih Tzu is depicted in artwork ranging from jewelry and ceramics to paintings.

of the Shih Tzu describes the breed's "dragon eyes, lion head, bear torso, frog mouth, palm leaf fan ears, rice teeth, elephant leg, feather duster tail, plum blossom paws, movement like a gold fish", and so on.

After Cixi's death in 1908, the kennels were dispersed and palace breeding became haphazard. Some breeding was still practiced by private individuals and specimens were exhibited, but the dogs were almost impossible to acquire. So far as is known, the breed became extinct in China after the Communist Revolution of 1949. China's new leaders considered the keeping of pet dogs, especially those identified with the former royal court, a corrupt symbol of wealth.

By this time, fortunately, a number of Shih Tzu had been brought home by diplomats who had been stationed in China and the breed was becoming established in Europe. The gene pool record of all existing Shih Tzu can be traced to only seven dogs and seven bitches. These fourteen include the Pekingese dog used in a known cross in England in 1952—a cross which caused considerable trouble, as it was done by a newcomer to the breed and reported after the fact. The other foundation dogs included three Shih Tzu imported from China that became the foundation of the Taishan kennel of Lady Brownrigg in England and six

additional imports to Great Britain between 1933 and 1959. Three other Shih Tzu were imported into Norway from China in 1932 by Mrs. Henrik Kauffman, including a bitch that was the only Shih Tzu bred in the Imperial Palace to reach the Western world, and a fourth was imported into Sweden by pioneer breeder Walter Ekman in the 1930s.

THE FOURTEEN FOUNDATION SHIH TZU

Hibou (black and white dog, parents unknown, imported into England from China in 1930 by Gen. Sir Douglas and Lady Brownrigg)

Shu-ssa (black and white bitch, parents unknown, imported into England from China in 1930 by Gen. Sir Douglas and Lady Brownrigg)

Lung-fu-ssu (black and white dog, parents unknown, imported into Ireland from China in 1930 by Miss E. M. Hutchins)

Aidzo (black and white dog born in Beijing in 1930, by Law hu x Lun Geni, imported from China into Norway in 1932 by Mrs. Henrik Kauffman)

Leidza (solid gold or brown bitch born in the Imperial Palace 1928, by Chin Tai x Wu Hai, imported from China into Norway in 1932 by Mrs. Henrik Kauffman; this is the only Shih Tzu specimen bred in the Imperial

Palace known to have contributed to today's Shih Tzu)

Schauder (black and white bitch born in Shanghai in 1931, by Aidzo-Huh x Hu-luh, imported from China into Norway in 1932 by Mrs. Henrik Kauffman)

Name unknown (Shih Tzu bitch imported from China into Sweden by Walter Ekman, the first breeder of Shih Tzu in Sweden, in 1934 or 1935)

Tashi of Chouette (liver bitch, by Fleury x Tashi Lumpi, inbred on Chinese imports Ming of Chouette and Hooza of Chouette, imported from Canada into England in 1938 by the Rt. Hon. the Earl of Essex)

Ming (black and white bitch, parents unknown, imported from China into England by Lt. Gen. Telfer-Smollett, Lord Lieutenant of Dunbartonshire)

Ishuh Tzu (gray brindle and white bitch, by Dandy of Shanghai x Chu-Chu of Shanghai, bred by Doreen Lennox in Shanghai and imported from China into England by Gen. Telfer-Smollet in 1948. Some experts feel that the Lhasa line was unknowingly introduced into English bloodlines through Ishuh

"Foo dog" sculptures have been popular for centuries.

Tzu, although the dog was examined in quarantine by Lady Brownrigg and declared suitable for registration as a Shih Tzu. Her dam was bred in the United States, where she was registered by the AKC as a Lhasa Apso under the name Hamilton Maru, and later went to Shanghai, where she was left for a time with Mrs. Lennox. At this time there was no clear delineation between the Chinese and Tibetan breeds in China, nor in the United States, where the Shih Tzu and Apso were still considered the same breed.)

Wuffles (solid gold or fawn dog, believed to have come from the kennel of Mr. Alfred Koehn in Peking, imported from China into England in 1948 by Mr. and Mrs. Fraser Buchanan)

Mai-ting (black and white bitch, parents unknown, imported from China into England in 1949 by Mr. and Mrs. Rowland Morris)

Hsi-li-ya (yellow and white bitch, parents unknown, imported from Hong Kong into England in 1952 by Mr. R. P. Dobson)

Philadelphus Suti-T'sun of Elfann (black and white purebred Pekingese dog, by Tong Wing of Alderbourne and Suti of Elfann, introduced by Miss E. M. Evans in England in 1952; four generations had to elapse, breeding back to pure Shih Tzu, before this line could be registered in England as purebred Shih Tzu, and the AKC required six generations).

Porcelain vase celebrating the Shih Tzu's heritage with colorful "Foo dogs."

SHIH TZU IN ENGLAND

British foundation stock is considered to include two additional dogs—Choo-Choo (Aidzo x Leidza), given to the British Queen Mother in 1933 by Mrs. Kauffman of Denmark, and Jungfaltets Jung-Ming, imported from Sweden by Mrs. M. Longden in 1959. Both dogs can be traced back to the original imports from China to Scandinavia.

The first English Shih Tzu were referred to as Tibetan Lion Dogs and classified as the same breed as the Apso, and the two were shown together. In 1934 the Tibetan Breed Association ruled that the Tibetan Lion Dogs were a separate breed and renamed them by the Chinese name for the breed, Shih Tzu. After this time, the breeds were judged separately and the Shih Tzu increased in popularity. By 1939, 183 Shih Tzu were registered with the Kennel Club. Shih Tzu were granted championship status by the Kennel Club in 1940, but breeding decreased dramatically during World War II and the breed's numbers declined. Only two Shih Tzu were registered in 1945, but by 1970 more than 1,000 Shih Tzu were being registered each year. In

Mai-Ting and Wuffles (with their daughter Pui-Yao) were among the last Shih Tzu to leave China.

1952 the controversial Pekingese cross was introduced in an effort to reduce size and length of leg and improve pigment. Dogs from the fourth generation of this cross were registered as purebred Shih Tzu by the Kennel Club.

Aidzo and Leidza, both born in Beijing, were owned by Mr. and Mrs. Henrik Kauffman. Leidza was the only dog among the original foundation stock who came from the Imperial Palace.

The first British Shih Tzu to earn its championship was Lady Brownrigg's bitch Ta-Chi of Taishan, in 1949. By late 1970, 65 Shih Tzu had earned their championships. The Shih Tzu Club, which had been founded in 1935, was later joined by a second club, the Manchu Shih Tzu Society. The latter organization, formed in 1956 as a private club favoring the smaller-type Shih Tzu, was recognized by the Kennel Club in 1962. The Manchu Shih Tzu Society was influential in revising the English breed standard to reduce the lowest permissible weight from 12 lb. to 9 lb. (later raised to 10 lb.).

The courtyard of the Imperial Palace in Beijing, where the Shih Tzu breed developed its distinctive style.

The English Standard for the Shih Tzu

(Adopted 1985. Note that the Shih Tzu in England is classified in the Utility Group – the British equivalent to the AKC Non-Sporting Group–rather than in the Toy Group as in the United States.)

General Appearance: Sturdy, abundantly coated dog with distinctly arrogant carriage and chrysanthemum-like face.

Characteristics: Intelligent, active and alert.

Head and Skull: Head broad, round, wide between eyes. Shock-headed with hair falling well over eyes. Good beard and whiskers, hair growing upwards on the nose, giving a distinctly chrysanthemum-like effect. Muzzle of ample width, square, short, not wrinkled, flat and hairy. Nose black, but dark liver in liver or liver-marked dogs, and about one inch from tip to definite stop. Nose level or slightly tip-tilted. Top of nose leather should be on a line with or slightly below lower eye rim. Wide-open nostrils. Down-pointed nose highly undesirable, as are pinched nostrils. Pigmentation on muzzle as unbroken as possible.

Eyes: Large, dark, round, placed well apart but not prominent. Warm expression. In liver or liver-marked dogs, lighter eye colour permissible. No white of eye showing.

Ears: Large, with long leathers, carried drooping. Set slightly below crown of skull, so heavily coated they appear to blend into hair of neck.

Mouth: Wide, slightly undershot or level. Lips level.

Neck: Well proportioned, nicely arched. Sufficient length to carry head proudly.

Forequarters: Shoulders well laid back. Legs short and muscular with ample bone, as straight as possible, consistent with broad chest being well let down.

Body: Longer between withers and root of tail than height at withers, well coupled and sturdy, chest broad and deep, shoulders firm, back level.

Hindquarters: Legs short and muscular with ample bone. Straight when viewed from the rear. Thighs well rounded and muscular. Legs looking massive on account of wealth of hair.

Feet: Rounded, firm and well padded, appearing big on account of wealth of hair.

The Lhasa Apso, originally bred as a watchdog in Tibet, is larger, longer on leg, and has a longer and narrower muzzle than the Shih Tzu.

The Shih Tzu combines certain characteristics of the Lhasa Apso and the Pekingese, standing midway between the two breeds in many particulars.

The Pekingese is the most extreme of the Oriental dogs, with the shortest muzzle and bowed, very short legs.

Tail: Heavily plumed carried fairly well over back. Set on high. Height approximately level with that of skull to give a balanced outline.

Gait/Movement: Arrogant, smooth-flowing, front legs reaching well forward, strong rear action and showing full pads.

Coat: Long, dense, not curly, with good undercoat. Slight wave permitted. Strongly recommended that hair on head be tied up.

Colour: All colours permissible, white blaze on forehead and white tip to tail highly desirable in parti-colours.

Weight and Size: 4.5-8.1 kg (10-18 lb.). Ideal weight 4.5-7.3 kg (10-16 lb.). Height at withers not more than 26.7 cm (10 1/2 in.), type and breed characteristics of utmost importance and on no account to be sacrificed to size alone.

Faults: Any departure from the foregoing points should be considered a fault, and the seriousness with which the fault should be regarded should be in exact proportion to its degree.

Note: *Male animals should have two apparently normal testicles fully descended into the scrotum.*

SHIH TZU IN SCANDINAVIA AND ELSEWHERE IN EUROPE

The first Scandinavian Shih Tzu were the three dogs imported into Norway by Mrs. Henrik Kauffman in 1932. These dogs, first registered with the Norwegian Kennel Club as Lhasa Terriers, were reregistered as Shih Tzu in 1939. These three dogs, plus possibly an unnamed Shih Tzu bitch imported into Sweden in the early 1930s, and their descendants were the foundation of the Scandinavian Shih Tzu. Tipsy, the first Shih Tzu in Denmark, was a son of Aidzo and Leidza, imported from Norway in 1939. The first litter whelped in Denmark, from a bitch imported from Norway in 1946, was bred by Astrid Jeppeson under her famous Bjorneholms prefix. Many of her dogs were later exported to Germany, Norway, the United States, and elsewhere, forming the foundation stock for such famous kennels as Erika Geusendam's Tschomo-Lungma kennel in Germany, Eta Pauptit's V. D. Oranje Manege kennel in the Netherlands, and Mr. and Mrs. C. O. Jungefeldt's Jungfaltets kennel in Sweden. Shih Tzu have long been bred and shown in France, Ger-many, and the Nether-lands and have been bred in the Czech Republic since the 1930s. The Shih Tzu breed was intro-duced into Fin-land in 1955 by two Swedish im-ports bred by Anna Hauffman.

This 1933 photo shows some of the early British imports and pioneer breeders: Lady Brownrigg with Hibou, Yangtse, and Shu-Ssa; Miss E. M. Hutchins with Lung-Fu-Ssu and Tang; and Sir Douglas Brownrigg with Hzu-Hsi.

Federation Cynologique Internationale Shih Tzu Standard

(This standard, approved in 1987, is used to judge Shih Tzu on the Continent, in South Africa, and in many countries in Asia and Latin America. Dogs winning FCI championship titles are referred to as International Champions.)

General Appearance: Sturdy, abundantly coated dog with distinctly arrogant carriage and chrysanthemum-like face.

Characteristics: Intelligent, active and alert.

Temperament: Friendly and independent.

Head and Skull: Head broad, round, wide between eyes. Shock-headed with hair falling well over eyes. Good beard and whiskers, hair growing upwards on the nose, giving a distinctly chrysanthemum-like effect. Muzzle of ample width, square, short, not wrinkled, flat and hairy. Nose black, but dark liver in liver or liver-marked dogs, and about one inch from tip to definite stop. Nose level or slightly tip-tilted. Top of nose level should be on a line with or slightly below lower eye rim. Wide-open nostrils. Down-pointed nose highly undesirable, as are pinched nostrils. Pigmentation on muzzle as unbroken as possible.

Eyes: Large, dark, round, placed well apart but not prominent. Warm expression. In liver or liver-marked dogs, lighter eye colour permissible. No white of eye showing.

Ears: Large, with long leathers, carried drooping. Set slightly below crown of skull, so heavily coated they appear to blend into hair of neck.

Mouth: Wide, slightly undershot or level. Lips level.

Neck: Well-proportioned, nicely arched. Sufficient length to carry head proudly.

Forequarters: Shoulders well laid back. Legs short and muscular with ample bone, as straight as possible, consistent with broad chest being well let down.

Body: Longer between withers and root of tail than height (at) withers, well coupled and sturdy, chest broad and deep, shoulders firm, back level.

Hindquarters: Legs short and muscular with ample bone. Straight when viewed from the rear. Thighs well rounded and muscular. Legs looking massive on account of wealth of hair.

Feet: Rounded, firm and well padded, appearing big on account of wealth of hair.

Tail: Heavily plumed, carried gaily well over back. Set on high. Height approximately level with that of skull to give a balanced outline.

Gait/Movement: Arrogant, smooth-flowing, front legs reaching well forward, strong rear action and showing full pads.

Coat: Long, dense, not curly, with good undercoat. Slight wave permitted. Strongly recommended that hair on head be tied up.

Colour: All colours permissible, white blaze on forehead and white tip to tail highly desirable in parti-colours.

Weight and Size: 4.5–8.1 kg (10–18 lb.). Ideal weight 4.5–7.3 kg (10–16 lb.). Height at withers not more than 26.7 cm ($10\frac{1}{2}$ in.), type and breed characteristics of the utmost importance and on no account to be sacrificed to size alone.

Faults: Any departure from the foregoing points should be considered a fault, and the seriousness with which the fault should be regarded should be in exact proportion to its degree.

Note: Male animals should have two apparently normal testicles fully descended into the scrotum.

Although dogs were passed back and forth from England to Scandinavia, there were certain general characteristics differentiating the early English and Scandinavian Shih Tzu. In general many (but certainly not all) English Shih Tzu tended to have heavier bones and larger heads; some strains tended to have curly coats, slightly bowed fronts, and undershot bites. Shih Tzu in Scandinavia generally tended to have straighter legs (called for in the FCI standard) and coats, more level toplines, and better bites, as a single missing tooth was cause to deny a dog a championship in much of Europe.

SHIH TZU AROUND THE WORLD

Most of the Shih Tzu in **Australia** come from Great Britain due to quarantine laws, and the Australian state kennel clubs are affiliated with the English Kennel Club. The first two U.S. Shih Tzu were imported into Australia in 1985. Showing in Australia is similar to showing in England. To earn a championship, a dog competes to earn Challenge points (5 for the Challenge Certificate itself plus one for every eligible dog entered, up to a maximum of 25 points per show, with 100 Challenge points won under at least four different judges required for a title). Both champions and non-champions are shown together, and Challenge Certificates can be and often are withheld if the judge feels the dog is not sufficiently outstanding to deserve to win the title of champion.

A contemporary rug sculpture depicting the Shih Tzu. (Phyllis Celmer for Gilbert Kahn)

The first Shih Tzu to be registered with the Kennel Union of **South Africa** was the Rhodesian-born Chien Lung in 1952. The first South African champion, in 1969, was Pei-Pei of Bollinridge. The number of Shih Tzu in South Africa has increased dramatically since the early 1980s, with imports coming from many European countries and the United States.

The nations of **Latin America** hold their dog shows under the regulations of the Federation Cynologique Internationale. Most of their foundation Shih Tzu were imported from the United States. The breed has become quite popular in such countries as Argentina.

Shih Tzu are one of the most popular breeds in **Japan**, which has an active Shih Tzu club. As early as 1976, a Shih Tzu specialty show in Osaka, Japan drew an entry of 63 Shih Tzu. Judging in Japan is similar to judging in the United States, although dogs and bitches do not compete against one another, and grooming skills are at an extremely high level.

Shih Tzu first reached the **Philippines** in the 1970s from Japan and England (and later the United States and Canada). The breed increased in popularity so rapidly that it ranked third in overall registrations by the late 1990s; the Philippine Shih Tzu Club held its first national specialty show in 1996. Shih Tzu were first shown in the Toy Group but were moved to the Non-Sporting Group in 1990. The system for earning a championship title in the Philippines is very much like that of the United States. Dogs can continue on to become Grand Champions through earning an additional 25 points by defeating other champions in winning Best of Breed or Best of Opposite Sex.

Thailand is another Asian nation where our breed has become very popular. Some Shih Tzu have also been exported to **China**, although the keeping of pet dogs remains against government regulations there. **Hong Kong's** quarantine restrictions have limited Shih Tzu imports, but the breed has many fanciers there. It is unclear what the fate of dogs there will be now that Hong Kong has been returned to Chinese rule.

The Shih Tzu in North America

SHIH TZU IN THE UNITED STATES

The first Shih Tzu were imported into the United States from England in the late 1930s, many of them by military personnel who had become familiar with the breed while stationed in England or Scandinavia. Before 1952 the Shih Tzu imports were reregistered with the American Kennel Club and shown and bred as Lhasa Apsos because the AKC did not recognize the Shih Tzu as a separate breed. After this time, the Shih Tzu was recognized as a distinct and separate breed; it gained admission to the Miscellaneous Class at dog shows in 1955.

Early U.S. Shih Tzu Imports Registered as Lhasa Apsos

Kota T'ang (bitch sired by Ching of the Mynd x Ting Tcheon of the Mynd; imported from England and registered with the AKC in 1937)

Wuffles of the Mynd (bitch by Ching of the Mynd x Ting of the Mynd, imported from England in 1938)

Ding-Ling of the Mynd (dog, littermate to Wuffles of the Mynd, also imported from England in 1938)

Yay Sih of Shebo (bitch imported from England and registered with the AKC in 1949; she became a Lhasa Apso champion)

Mai-Ling of Boydon (bitch imported from England by Yangtze of Taishan x Hseuh-li Chan of Taishan; registered with the AKC as a Lhasa Apso in 1943)

Lindli-lu (English import bitch born 1946; AKC Lhasa Apso registration number R64026)

Linyi of Lhakang (English import bitch born 1948, daughter of Lindli-lu; AKC Lhasa Apso registration number R64027)

Fardale Fu-ssi (English import bitch by Pu of Oulton x Mu-chi of Lhakang; AKC registered in 1948, she became a Lhasa champion)

Chu Chu of Shanghai (dam of Chinese import English foundation Ishuh Tzu, registered as a Lhasa Apso by the AKC under the name Hamilton Maru. She won Best of Breed at the Westminster Kennel Club. She had been bred by Suydam Cutting of Hilton Farms in New Jersey and was four generations removed from two Apsos given to him in about 1930 by the 13th Dalai Lama. She later went to Shanghai with a Commander Doyle and was left there for a time with Mrs. Lennox.)

The Early Days

Once the breed gained separate status, a dedicated group of U.S. fanciers began to popularize the Shih Tzu. Maureen Murdock and Philip Price, her nephew, were the first to import and breed Shih Tzu registered as such in the United States. In 1954 Mr. Price brought back to the United States from England Golden S. Wen of Chasmu. The first purebred Shih Tzu born in the United States may have been a litter of three bred by Price out of his English imported bitch, Ho-Lai-Sheum. Price also exhibited the first Shih Tzu at the 1957 Kennel

Club of Philadelphia show. The breed was shown for the first time at the prestigious Westminster Kennel Club show in 1961, where the Miscellaneous Class entry consisted of five Shih Tzu (four owned by Ingrid Colwell and one by Maureen Murdock) and one Akita. The first Shih Tzu ever to be shown by a professional handler in the United States was Jo-Nil-Pih-Heh of Telota, owned by Richard Bauer and handled by Anne Hone Rogers (now Anne Rogers Clark) at the 1962 Westminster Kennel Club show.

The first champion bitch to be imported into the United States was French Ch. Jungfaltets Jung-Wu, a 9-lb. gold and white, in 1960. Ingrid Colwell bought her in her native Sweden and showed her to her championship in France while her Air Force husband was stationed there. Ingrid arrived in the United States with five Shih Tzu, including two with the Pukedals prefix (her mother's kennel name in Sweden). From 1960 to 1968, when Ingrid sadly died in a fire, she imported

Ingrid Colwell with some of her Shih Tzu. Mrs. Colwell was the individual perhaps most responsible for popularizing our breed in the United States.

several Shih Tzu from both Scandinavia and England. She was the individual perhaps most responsible for popularizing the breed in the U.S., both because of her enthusiasm and because of her firsthand knowledge of the breed in Europe. Before her death she had bred 79 Shih Tzu, enough to help establish the breed in the United States.

Yvette Duval, a close friend of Ingrid's, imported the first male champion, French Ch. Pukedals Ding Dang. Yvette bought this black and white male from Ingrid's mother and finished his championship in France before her Air Force husband Lucian was reassigned to the United States. The Duvals also brought two Shih Tzu bitches into the country with them.

Ch. Bjorneholms Pif, imported to the United States from Denmark by Jack and Mary Wood in 1968, was the first U.S. champion of our breed. He had previously earned championship titles in Denmark, Germany, Switzerland, Belgium, and Czechoslovakia.

More Early U.S. Breeders of Shih Tzu

Mrs. Noel Alford (Loo Wi)

Jay Ammon and Sue Kaufman (Jaisu)

Dr. and Mrs. Sidney Bashore (Shu Lin)

Mr. and Mrs. Jack Coleman (Coleman)

Mrs. Eloise Craig (Good Time)

Mrs. J. D. Curtice (Jo-Wil)

Theresa Drimal (Silver Nymph)

Benton E. Dudgeon (Mogene)

Patricia Semones Durham (Pasha, Si-Kiang)

Rev. and Mrs. D. Allan Easton (Chumulari)

Rae Eckes (House of Wu)

Margaret Edel (Mar-Del)

Jane Fitts (Encore)

Mrs. John Foreman (Foreman)

Jean Gadberry (Lakoya)

Mrs. Dorothy Gagnon (Gagnon)

Mr. and Mrs. Charles T. Gardner (La-Mi)

Mrs. Edith Groves (Jonedith)

G. F. Houston (Judlu)

Mrs. Joyce Larson (Hasu)

Bill and Joan Kibler (Taramont)

Col. and Mrs. James E. Lett (Tamworth)

Col. and Mrs. Frank Loob (Zijuh)

Pat Michael (Sangchen)

Will Mooney (Bill-Ora)

Edith Norton (Nor-tons)

Col. and Mrs. Robert Olinger (Olinger)

Mrs. Brenda Ostencio (Kwan Yin)

Richard Paisley (Paisley)

Barbara Pennington (Copper Penny)

Mr. and Mrs. Eugene Reynolds (Reynolds)

Thelma Ruth (Stonyacres)

Florence and Louis Sanfilippo (Char-Nick)

Dr. and Mrs. George Schoel (Hee Shee's)

Lynne Seydel (Mai-Lyn)

Joel Strange (Str-range)

Bruna Stubblefield (Beedoc)

Ann Hickok Warner (Rosemar)

Jack and Mary Wood (Mariljac)

By 1961 there were more than 100 Shih Tzu registered in the United States, both imports and offspring born here. With much pleasure and always a great deal of fun, many early Shih Tzu lovers showed their best all over the country in an effort to popularize the breed and gain full AKC recognition. They were stopped by all kinds of curious people and answered questions at shows all day long. Many of them sold dogs to people new to the breed, thus spreading the joy of owning a Shih Tzu and helping to educate others about this relatively new breed to the United States. In 1962, when there was still a Miscellaneous Class held at Westminster, there were twice as many Shih Tzu entered as in 1961.

Ingrid Colwell and owned by the Rev. and Mrs. D. Allan Easton. Best of Opposite Sex was Colwell's Swedish import Fr. Ch. Jungfaltets Jung Wu. By 1968, there were local Shih Tzu clubs for the New York-Upper New Jersey-Connecticut area, Maryland, Wisconsin, Illinois, Texas, Southern California, and Northern California.

I can personally attest to the fact that showing Shih Tzu in the early days was much different than it is today. We didn't know about things like ironing coats—or even much about putting up topknots or trimming—and we drove for hundreds of

Chumulari Ying-Ying, a Pif son, won Best in Show on the first day Shih Tzu were eligible to compete for championship points. This was the first time a dog of any breed had ever won Best in Show on the first day of AKC breed recognition.

By July 1965 there were 724 Shih Tzu registered with the American Shih Tzu Club, and registrations had spread rather nicely across the United States. Some folks were starting to form local Shih Tzu clubs, and what is believed to be the first Shih Tzu fun match, sponsored by the Penn-Ohio Shih Tzu Club, was held on June 27, 1964, at Ingrid Colwell's home in Middletown, PA. While there were only about 400 Shih Tzu in the entire country, the match drew an entry of 50, from seven states. Best Adult in Match was Si-Kiang's Tashi, a black bitch bred by

miles in hopes of winning at best a pink ribbon (first in Miscellaneous Class) in direct competition with Akitas, Cavalier King Charles Spaniels, and the rest. But there was a wonderful feeling of camaraderie in those days as breeders and handlers shared their knowledge with the newcomers. Most Shih Tzu then were owner-handled and lived as house pets, an era many of us hated to see end, much as we wanted to be able to earn championships and compete for Group and Best in Show wins. What today we would consider a lack of grooming skills made it much easier to see just what was beneath all that hair, particularly in terms of the head.

The Breed in the U.S. After Recognition

The AKC opened its Stud Book to the breed on March 16, 1969. On September 1, 1969, when Shih Tzu were shown for the first time in the United States for championship points, the Easton's Chumulari Ying Ying won Best in Show in New Brunswick, New Jersey. That same day his father, Bjorneholm's Pif, owned by Mary Wood and Norman Patton, won the Toy Group in Bloomington, Illinois, while a Pif granddaughter, Lakoya Princess Tanya Shu, owned by Jean Gadberry, won the Toy Group in Eugene, Oregon. Already a champion in five European countries, Pif became the first U.S. Shih Tzu champion by winning three five-point majors in 13 days. The first U.S. champion Shih Tzu bitch was the Easton's Ch. Chumulari Hih-Hih. Between September 1, 1969 and December 31, 1970, 100 Shih Tzu champions were recorded by the AKC. These included not only dogs bred in the United States but also many imports, primarily from Canada, England, Scandinavia as well as Germany, the Netherlands, and Australia. That same year, the first that Shih Tzu were eligible to compete at the Westminster Kennel Club show, Ying Ying won the Breed over an entry of 27 Shih Tzu.

The breed gained rapidly in popularity after AKC recognition, but at first it exhibited wide variations in size and type. Within about five years, however, size had become fairly well stabilized, with most exhibits in the 10-to-15-lb. range. Breeders also worked hard to breed better coats, level toplines, straighter fronts, and improved movement. Over the years, the breed in the United States (and in Canada, where it developed along similar lines) became not only more uniform but also more elegant. One of the most memorable specialties ever, for those of us who've been around that long, was the 1976 specialty, held in conjunction with the Shih Tzu Fanciers of Greater Miami. Before his death, the late Shih Tzu handler Dee Shepherd said that simply surviving the cut in the BOB class at this specialty was one of the biggest thrills of his life; the entry read like a who's who of Shih Tzudom, and the opportunity to have one's dogs judged by England's Elfreda M. Evans and Sweden's Erna Jungefeldt, who were among the pioneers of the breed, drew a world record entry of 186 Shih Tzu (273 entries). At the Miami specialty on the following day, the ladies reversed their assignments, so that each had the opportunity to judge every dog.

Many of the changes that occurred during the 20 years after breed recognition were reflected in the revised Shih Tzu breed standard adopted in 1989, which spelled out the attributes of the ideal Shih Tzu in much greater detail than had the 1969 standard.

In 1992, Ch. Lainee Sigmund Floyd ROM was voted most influential stud dog in the history of the breed by the members of the American Shih Tzu Club. (Elaine Meltzer)

While modern dogs are much more elegant, and fronts have improved greatly since the early days, the breed still can stand improvement. The greatest problem by the late 1990s seemed to be tall, long-legged Shih Tzu lacking substance proportionate to their size and, more distressing, a deterioration in the quality of the headpiece. Too many contemporary Shih Tzu, many long-time breeder-judges observe, are losing the large, dark, round eyes that give the breed its unique and desirable warm expression. Also, heads seem to fall away much too quickly above the eye, the eyes are becoming smaller, and

In 1993, Ch. Tu Chu's Mesmerized ROM was voted most influential brood bitch in the history of the breed by the members of the American Shih Tzu Club. (Gilbert photo; Kathy Kwait)

many eyes are showing far too much white. Much of this could be a natural reversion to normal canine structure and indicates that breeders must take care to breed to the exaggerated heads called for in the breed standard if the Shih Tzu head type is to be maintained.

There are many stud dogs and brood bitches that have had a tremendous impact on the breed over the years since recognition. Many of them became ASTC National Specialty Best of Breed winners and holders of the coveted ASTC Registry of Merit.

Two individual Shih Tzu, however, deserve special mention. In 1992 and 1993, at the request of the American Kennel Club, the ASTC membership was polled and asked to vote for the stud dog and brood bitch that they felt had been most influential in the history of the breed. Ch. Lainee Sigmund Floyd ROM was voted most influential stud dog of the past. Although never shown in an all-breed show after completing his championship, he was the sire of 69 U.S. and 30 foreign champions and was top-producing

Shih Tzu for 1980, 1981, and 1982. He and his get amassed numerous specialty wins, and his offspring were particularly noted for their lovely heads, sweet expressions, short backs, soundness, and overall balance. It was his prepotency for these qualities (emphasized even more in the 1989 Shih Tzu standard than in the one under which he and most of his get competed) that made his impact on the breed today so significant. The brood bitch winner, Ch. Tu Chu's Mesmerized ROM, had at that time produced 10 champions (an extraordinary number for a bitch of a Toy breed) and was tied for number three all-time top-producing Shih Tzu bitch. (She subsequently produced additional champions.) Six of her offspring had also been awarded ROMs for producing the requisite number of champions, and her name appears in the pedigrees of many of today's top-winning Shih Tzu, although she and most of her get were never specialed. She stamped her type on her descendants in breedings to several different dogs—the real test of a great producer of either sex.

THE SHIH TZU IN CANADA

The first Shih Tzu in Canada (which included a pair of dogs imported from Shanghai in 1931 by Mrs. J. E. Wheeler and later owned by Margaret Torrible of British Columbia and three Shih Tzu imported from Beijing, England and Czechoslovakia by Mr. and Mrs. Patrick Morgan) were registered as Lhasa Terriers, as in the United States. A bitch of Mrs. Morgan's breeding, Tashi of Chouette, was later exported to Lady Brownrigg in England. The Shih Tzu registry opened in 1934 but virtually died out during World War II. The Shih Tzu gained recognition as a separate breed of that name in Canada in 1952. The first Shih Tzu registered by the Canadian Kennel Club was Ah Sid of Lhakang, in that year. King Chan of Clarebrand, a brindle and white dog of English Elfann and Lhakang bloodlines, became the first Canadian Shih Tzu Champion in 1959. Shih Tzu in Canada thus were able to compete for championship titles several years before the breed gained full recognition in the United States.

The Canadian Shih Tzu Club was founded in 1973 with Jeffrey Carrique as president. Mr. Carrique and his wife did much to promote the breed in Canada and the United States. Their Am-Can-Bda. Ch. Carrimount Ah-Chop-Chop ROM was the first Canadian-bred Shih Tzu to become the top-winning Shih Tzu in the United States in 1971. The other founding members were Mr. and Mrs. A. Alex Cattanach, Mr. and Mrs. Keith Johnstone, and Mr. and Mrs. Andrew Dickson. The first Canadian Shih Tzu specialty was held in 1975, in conjunction with the United Kennel Club show in Montreal; there was an entry of 37 dogs. Since that time specialty shows have been held annually in various locations in Canada. The Canadian Shih Tzu Club was recognized by the Canadian Kennel Club in 1979. In addition to its newsletter, the club also published *Canadian Shih Tzu Club History to 1987* (1988), which contains much useful information about the breed in Canada.

Exhibiting in Canada

Many U.S. Shih Tzu have earned Canadian championships, and vice versa, and the American Shih Tzu Club has many Canadian members. If you wish to exhibit your Shih Tzu in Canada, contact the Canadian Kennel Club (89 Skyway Avenue, Etobicoke, Ontario, Canada M9W 6R4) for its memo designed for U.S. residents about showing in Canada.

Although dogs can be shown in Canada without CKC registration, you must pay an additional listing fee with each show entry for unregistered dogs or dogs without an Event Registration Number (ERN). Also, you cannot receive any Canadian title your dog may earn until it has an ERN number or is registered with the CKC, and your dog cannot move up to compete in the champions-only class until it has an ERN number or has been CKC registered. Request an application for an ERN or a foreign-dog registration for a U.S. resident. To obtain an ERN you may send a photocopy of your AKC registration papers and the appropriate fee to the CKC by mail or FAX. To obtain a CKC registration (required for Shih Tzu who will be bred and whose offspring will be registered in Canada), you will need to submit your original AKC registration certificate, an original AKC three-generation pedigree, a microchip or a tattoo registration, and the required fee. Microchips can be purchased from the CKC, which alternately can provide you with a tattoo registration number.

To earn a Canadian championship, your dog must earn 10 points under three different judges. "Major" wins are not required. Unlike in the United States, the point schedule is the same throughout the country for every breed. One point is awarded to the Winners Dog or Bitch if there are two dogs of that sex in competition; two points when there are three to five dogs in competition, three points for six to nine dogs, four points for ten to twelve dogs, and five points for thirteen or more dogs. Best of Winners is awarded points based on the number of dogs defeated in both sexes combined. Extra points may be awarded for Group placements, but no dog may win more than 5 points at any one show. Canadian dog shows also offer separate competition for puppies leading to Best Puppy in Show; one entry fee covers both competitions for puppies.

Size: The Shih Tzu is not a Toy dog. This is a smaller type of dog with good bone and substance. Height at withers approximately 9 to 10 1/2 inches (23-27 cm). Breed type and balance always to be main consideration.

One special feature of Canadian shows is breed, group, and Best in Show competition for puppies. (Alex Smith for Wendy and Richard Paquette)

Canadian Shih Tzu Standard

(Note: Shih Tzu in Canada are shown in the Non-Sporting Group.)

Origin and Purpose: The Shih Tzu was developed in the palaces of China from Tibetan temple dogs crossed with other Chinese breeds. It was originally bred to be a companion and that remains its sole purpose today. Sturdy and surprisingly hardy, they are well suited to both city and country living.

General Appearance: The Shih Tzu is an abundantly coated dog with a distinctly Oriental appearance. It is a solid, sound little dog that is rather heavy for its size.

Temperament: Shih Tzu are distinctly arrogant with a character all their own. They are exceptionally good-natured, affectionate and intelligent. They are full of life and have an air of importance that cannot be denied.

Coat and Colour: A luxurious, long, flowing coat with an undercoat. May be slightly wavy but never curly. The coat may be parted from the root of the tail to the back of the skull. The hair on the head may be tied up to form a topknot. A bow or ribbon to be optional. Coat may be trimmed so as not to interfere with the movement of the dog. All colours are acceptable providing they have black noses, lips and eye rims. The exceptions are the livers and blues, which have pigmentation that compliments that particular colour.

Head: Skull round, broad and wide between the eyes with a definite stop. The muzzle is short, square and about one-fifth of the total length of the skull. The muzzle is approximately 1 inch (2 $\frac{1}{2}$ cm) from the stop to the tip of the nose. The upward sweep of the front part of the muzzle should place the nose level with the bottom of the eye. The placement of the muzzle is directly responsible for the nose placement, which may be slightly tilted or level. The nose leather should be broad and the nostrils well open. Eyes should be large, dark and round, except in livers and blues where the light colour is permissible. The eyes should be well set in the skull and the expression should be warm and irresistible. Ear leathers drooping, set just below the crown of the head and so heavily coated that they appear to blend with hair of the neck. Mouth is slightly undershot or level, the bottom jaw is wide and strong. Teeth should not be visible when the mouth is closed.

Neck: The neck must be in balance with the body length and must also complement the high tail set and carriage.

Forequarters: Shoulders well developed, muscular and well set to allow freedom of movement. The upper arm well laid back thus allowing for the desired width and depth forming a good forechest. The legs straight, well boned, set well under the body and fitting closely to the chest. Feet moderate size and well padded.

Body: This is not a square dog. The length of the back from the withers to the tail set to be slightly longer than the height from the withers to the ground. Taking into consideration the forechest as well as the area behind the tail, the Shih Tzu should appear rectangular in outline. The body should be deep, sturdy and well coupled with a good spring of rib. There should be little or no tuckup of the underline. A good forechest is essential to both the movement and balance of the Shih Tzu. The topline should be level both standing and moving.

Hindquarters: Strong, muscled, well angulated and in balance with forequarters.

Hocks short, sturdy and turning neither in nor out. Feet moderate size and well padded.

Tail: Well feathered, set high and carried gaily over the back in a loose curve with the tip just touching the back.

Gait: Should be smooth and flowing with the head and tail held high. Extension both front and rear. Front legs should move out of the coat in a straight line, feet turning neither in nor out. Rear legs show strong rear action displaying full pads on the move. The Shih Tzu has a distinct swagger when on the move that is enhanced by his air of importance.

Faults: Temperament—Any deviation from the above-mentioned temperament to be considered very undesirable. Size—Lack of proper bone and substance. Coat and Colour—Excessive trimming, sparse or wooly coats, missing pigmentation. Head—Narrow head, lack of stop, pink on nose or eye rims, small or light-coloured eyes, eye white showing, missing canines or incisors, lack of strength of underjaw, pinched nostrils, wry mouths, tongue showing when the mouth is closed, wrinkles like a Peke. Neck—Too short in that it does not complement the carriage and outline of the Shih Tzu. Forequarters—Excessive legginess and crooked legs. Body—Lack of forechest, narrow, weedy bodies with no bone and substance, high in rear standing or moving. Shih Tzu not adhering to the correct rectangular outline. Hindquarters—Slipping stifles and luxating hocks, cow hocks. Tail—Tails flat on back, pig tails, tails not carried gaily or happily, tails carried sickle like without tip touching back. Gait—Lack of reach and drive, bouncing gait, inability to move with tail or head held high.

Disqualifications: Scissors or overshot bites, one or two blue eyes.

The American Shih Tzu Club, Inc.

There were very few Shih Tzu in the United States when the American Kennel Club accepted the Shih Tzu into the Miscellaneous Class in 1955. As with all unrecognized breeds, complete records of imports and births had to be kept by individuals or groups until such time as a breed club was formed and a registrar selected. This was extremely important if a breed hoped to earn full recognition by the American Kennel Club and be able to compete for AKC championships. Because the early Shih Tzu supporters and enthusiasts were so spread out across the country, the early Shih Tzu clubs were formed independently of each other. The first was the Shih Tzu Club of America, founded in the eastern part of the United States in 1957. By 1960 two additional Shih Tzu organizations, the Texas Shih Tzu Society and a group in Florida headed by a Mr. Curtis had been formed by other individuals who shared a common interest in, love for, and commitment to the Shih Tzu breed.

In 1963 the Shih Tzu Club of America and the Texas Shih Tzu Society merged to form the American Shih Tzu Club (ASTC), which was incorporated in 1968. The two clubs combined their records into a single registry. This registry, which contained information on 369 Shih Tzu in July 1963, had grown to include 1,544 Shih Tzu by July 1967. The keeping of correct up-to-date records on all imports and births was a very important task during the years leading up to AKC recognition, as was the role of its members in arousing interest in the breed by showing their dogs throughout the country. If interest in the breed had not increased, the AKC could have withdrawn the Miscellaneous status for the breed. Between 1963 and 1969, the ASTC had three registrars: Lucian Duval, Gene Dudgeon (publisher of the now-defunct *Shih Tzu News*), and Mary Wood. By 1969, the ASTC registry contained data on about 3,000 dogs.

The ASTC had originally adopted the English breed standard for the Shih Tzu, but the AKC felt that some matters in this standard needed clarification, and a standard revision committee was appointed. In 1969 the AKC accepted a revised breed standard that had been approved by the ASTC board of directors. On March 16, 1969, the Shih Tzu officially became the 116th AKC-recognized breed, eligible to compete for AKC championships effective September 1, 1969, and the AKC assumed the task of keeping breed records. The dogs in the ASTC registry, plus those in the independent registry maintained by Mr. Curtis, were registered by the AKC at this time, and the AKC Stud Book was closed for the registration of Shih Tzu foundation stock on June 30, 1970.

Since then, the ASTC has continued to grow in membership, in local Shih Tzu club affiliates, and in liaisons with other Shih Tzu organizations throughout the world. The ASTC is a member club of the American Kennel Club. It held three Sanctioned A match shows (in 1970 in Terre Haute, IN; in 1971 in San Antonio, TX; and in 1972 in Trenton, NJ) before being approved for the first ever AKC-licensed Shih Tzu specialty show, held in Portland, OR, in 1973. National specialties have been held annually since that time across the United States.

A study of the photographs of national specialty Best in Show winners gives a good overview of how breed type has changed in the years since recognition.

Portland, Oregon, 1973
Ch. Long's Bedeviled Bedazzled (Janet Long)

Marlborough, Massachusetts, 1974
CH. CHAR-NICK'S BE-WIT-CHING OF COPA

Houston, Texas, 1975
CH. DRAGONWYCK THE GREAT GATSBY ROM
(MARTIN BOOTH)

Miami, Florida, 1976
CH. V. I. P. CONFUCIOUS (CLARK)

St. Louis, Missouri, 1977
CH. LOU WAN CASINOVA ROM (ASHBEY)

New Carrollton, Maryland, 1978
Ch. Afshi's Gunther ROM (Allen Ellsworth)

Long Beach, California, 1979
Ch. Ying Su Johnie Reb ROM (Missy Yuhl)

Miami, Florida, 1980
Ch. Jolei Chinese Checker ROM (Ritter)

Dallas, Texas, 1981
Ch. Luken's All Fired Up ROM (Graham)

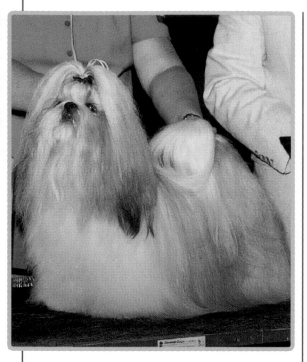

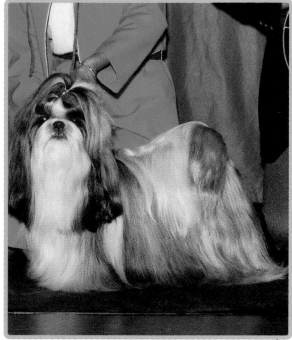

Trevose, Pennsylvania, 1982
CH. FANCEE HEIR MHALE BON D'ART ROM
(ASHBEY)

San Mateo, California, 1983
Romulus, Michigan, 1986
CH. LOU WAN REBEL ROUSER ROM (CALLEA)

Worcester, Massachusetts, 1984
CH. WEN SHU'S MONA LISA
(MOMENTS BY JANE)

Beaverton, Oregon, 1985
Fort Worth, Texas, 1987
CH. CABRAND AGENT ORANGE V LOU WAN
ROM (BOBBI)

New Carrollton, Maryland, 1988
Princeton, New Jersey, 1990
CH. SHENTE'S BRANDY ALEXANDER ROM
(BRUCE K. HARKINS)

Ontario, California, 1989
CH. SNOBHILL'S FREE LANCE CD, ROM
(MISSY YUHL)

Portland, Oregon,1991
NAYSMITH JOLEI JACKPOT ROM (CALLEA PHOTO)

Romulus, Michigan, 1992
CH. MAHAL'S AMADEUS MOZART ROM (BOOTH)

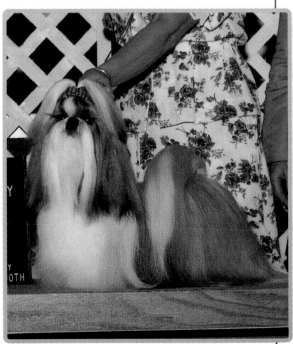

Millbrae, California, 1993 - Miami, Florida, 1994
CH. SHENTE'S JOLEI IN YOUR DREAMS ROM (PAULETTE)

Salt Lake City, Utah, 1995
CH. KEEPSAKE'S DREAM CATCHER (MISSY YUHL)

Seacaucus, New Jersey, 1998
CH. CHARING CROSS RAGTIME COWBOY
(TOM DIGIACOMO)

Minneapolis, Minnesota, 1996
CH. GRENOVILLE RAINBOWS END (OLSON PHOTO BY TERI)

Burbank, California, 1997
CH. BESWICKS IN THE NICK OF TIME (HOLLOWAY PHOTO)

THE BREED STANDARD

The ASTC remains the official guardian of the U.S. breed standard for the Shih Tzu, which describes the ideal specimen of the breed and is used by both dog show judges and breeders in determining the quality of an individual Shih Tzu. Any changes in this standard must be approved by the general membership of the ASTC. The ASTC believes that any Shih Tzu which is not a good representative of the breed according to the standard should not be bred, and that the sole goal of breeding should be to improve breed quality. The current breed standard (the first revision since breed recognition) was approved on May 9, 1989. You may wish to compare the 1969 standard with the standard used today.

1969 Shih Tzu Breed Standard
(with 1989 Standard revisions italics in parentheses)

GENERAL APPEARANCE: Very active, lively and alert, with a distinctly arrogant carriage. The Shih Tzu is proud of bearing as befits his noble *(Chinese)* ancestry *(as a highly valued, prized companion and palace pet),* and walks with head well up and tail carried gaily over the back. *(Although there has always been considerable size variation, the Shih Tzu must be compact, solid, carrying good weight and substance. Even though a toy dog, the Shih Tzu must be subject to the same requirements of soundness and structure prescribed for all breeds, and any deviations from the ideal described in the standard should be penalized to the extent of the deviation. Structural faults common to all breeds are as undesirable in the Shih Tzu as in any other breed, regardless of whether or not such faults are specifically mentioned in the standard.)*

HEAD: Broad and round, wide between the eyes *(its size in balance with the overall size of dog being neither too large nor too small. Expression: Warm, sweet, wide-eyed, friendly and trusting. An overall well-balanced and pleasant expression supercedes the importance of individual parts. Care* should be taken to look and examine well beyond the hair to determine if what is seen is the actual head and expression rather than an image created by grooming technique.) Muzzle square and short, but not wrinkled *(with good cushioning),* about one inch from tip of nose to stop **(changed to: *Ideally, no longer than one inch from tip of nose to stop, although length may vary slightly in relation to overall size of dog. Front of muzzle should be flat; lower lip and chin not protruding and definitely never receding).* Definite stop. Eyes: Large, dark and round but not prominent, *(looking straight ahead; very dark, Lighter on liver pigmented dogs and blue pigmented dogs),* placed well apart. Eyes should show warm expression. Ears: Large, with long leathers, and carried drooping; set slightly below the crown of the skull; so heavily coated that they appear to blend with the hair of the neck. Teeth: level or slightly undershot bite. **(changed to:** *Jaw: Undershot. Jaw is broad and wide. A missing tooth or slightly misaligned teeth should not be too severely penalized. Teeth and tongue should not show when mouth is closed. Nose: Nostrils are broad, wide, and open.)*

FOREQUARTERS: Legs short, straight, well boned, muscular, *(set well-apart and under chest, with elbows set close to body)* and heavily coated. Legs and feet look massive on account of the wealth of hair. *(Shoulders: Well-angulated, well-laid back, well laid-in, fitting smoothly into body.)*

BODY: Body between the withers and the root of the tail is somewhat **(changed to** *slightly)* longer than the height at the withers; well **(changed to** short) coupled and sturdy *(with no waist or tuckup).* Chest broad and deep, shoulders firm, back level. *(Of utmost importance is an overall well-balanced dog with no exaggerated features. Neck: Well set-on, flowing smoothly into shoulders; of sufficient length to permit natural high head carriage and in balance with height and length of dog.)*

HINDQUARTERS: Legs, short, well boned and muscular, are straight when viewed from the rear *(with well-bent stifles, not* close set but in line with forequarters. Hocks: *Well let down, perpendicular).* Thighs well rounded and muscular. Legs look massive on account of wealth of hair. *(Angulation of hindquarters should be in balance with forequarters.)*

FEET: Of good size, firm, well padded, *(point straight ahead)* with hair between the pads. Dewclaws, if any, on the hind legs are generally removed. Dewclaws on the forelegs may be removed.

TAIL: Heavily plumed and curved well over the back; carried gaily, set on high. *(Too loose, too tight, too flat, or too low set a tail is undesirable and should be penalized to extent of deviation.)*

COAT: A luxurious, *(double-coated)* long, dense *(and flowing)* coat. May be slightly wavy but not curly. Good wooly undercoat. The hair on top of the head may be tied up. *(Trimming: Feet, bottom of coat, and anus may be done for neatness and to facilitate movement. Fault: Excessive trimming.)*

COLOR: All colors permissible *(and to be considered equally).* Nose and eye rims black, except that dogs with liver markings may have liver noses and slightly lighter eyes.

GAIT: Slightly rolling, smooth and flowing, with strong rear action. ***(changed to*** *The Shih Tzu moves straight and must be shown at its own natural speed, neither raced nor strung-up, to evaluate its smooth, flowing, effortless movement with good front reach and equally strong rear drive, level top line, naturally high head carriage, and tail carried in gentle curve over back.)*

SIZE: Height at withers—9 to 10 $\frac{1}{2}$ inches—should be no more than 11 inches nor less than 8 inches. Weight of mature dogs—12 to 15 pounds—should be no more than 18 pounds nor less than 9 pounds. ***(changed to*** *Ideal weight: 9 to 16 pounds.)* However, type and breed characteristics are of the greatest importance. ***(changed to*** *The Shih Tzu must never be so high stationed as to appear leggy, nor so low stationed as to appear dumpy or squatty. Regardless of size, the Shih Tzu is always compact, solid and carries good weight and substance.)*

FAULTS: Narrow head, overshot bite, snippiness, pink on nose *(lips)* or eye rims, small or light eyes, legginess, sparse coat, lack of definite stop *(hyperextension of hocks, excessive trimming, close-set eyes, excessive eye white, single coat, curly coat).*

(TEMPERAMENT: As the sole purpose of the Shih Tzu is that of a companion and house pet, it is essential that its temperament be outgoing, happy, affectionate, friendly and trusting towards all.)

ASTC CODE OF ETHICS

The ASTC has a code of ethics approved by its members. If you apply for membership in the ASTC, you must agree to abide by this code.

1. I agree to follow the regulations as set forth by the American Kennel Club as they pertain to my purebred dog operations.

2. I agree to abide by and uphold the principles of the Constitution and By-Laws and this Code of Ethics of the American Shih Tzu Club, Inc.

3. I will furnish a signed registration application, transfer or AKC limited registration certificate and three-generation pedigree with each puppy sold. I may have a written agreement with the purchaser at the time of sale that papers will be withheld.

4. I will encourage spaying or neutering of animals not desirable for breeding.

5. I will not sell my puppies to pet shops or commercial pet mill establishments, nor will I donate puppies for raffles or auctions.

6. I will not crossbreed or advertise for sale puppies that have been crossbred.

7. I will not give stud service to unregistered bitches.

8. I will advise the purchaser of my puppy to have the puppy checked by a veterinarian within 2 days (48 hours) of the sale (additional time allowed if the puppy is sold on a Friday or Saturday). I will refund the purchase price or take the puppy back and replace it if it is found to be unfit by a veterinarian.

9. Except for unusual situations, I will not sell my puppies at less than twelve weeks of age.

10. I will maintain the best possible standard of health and care in all of my dogs and see that puppies are immunized and checked for parasites. I will furnish complete health records, care, feeding, and grooming instructions with each puppy sold.

11. I will attempt to sell my pet puppies within the range of other breeders in my area.

12. In my breeding program I will keep alert for and work to control and/or eradicate inherited problems and conditions that are particular to my breed, and breed as closely as possible to the standard of the breed.

13. I will represent my dogs as honestly as possible to prospective buyers and try to assist the serious novice in his understanding of the breed.

14. I will try at all times to show good sportsmanship and keep in mind that the good of the breed comes before any personal benefits.

15. I will refrain from deceptive or erroneous advertising.

ASTC ACTIVITIES AND PUBLICATIONS

The ASTC conducts a national specialty show each year, where members and friends of our breed can meet, attend various educational programs, and see Shih Tzu from all over the country. The location of the national specialty show varies from year to year. Many ASTC local club affiliates hold their own specialty shows, which the ASTC supports.

Since 1978, the ASTC has also compiled a Registry of Merit (ROM). Special awards, called Register of Merit, are presented annually to ASTC member-owned Shih Tzu dogs that have produced six or more AKC champions and bitches that have produced four or more AKC champions. Other ASTC annual awards include Top-Winning Shih Tzu owned by an ASTC member, Best of Opposite Sex to Top-Winning Shih Tzu, and Breeder awards for each of these; Top-Producing Stud Dog, Top-Producing Brood Bitch, and Breeder awards for each of these; Top-Winning Obedience Shih Tzu; and Highest-Scoring Agility Shih Tzu.

ASTC members conduct judges' and breeders' seminars throughout the country, most commonly in conjunction with national and local Shih Tzu specialty shows. The ASTC also encourages its members to become involved in obedience, agility, pet therapy, and other such activities.

As the future of our wonderful breed depends upon responsible breeding practices, the ASTC strongly encourages its members and the general public to conduct health screening and testing of all breeding stock. The ASTC has three committees specifically involved in the area of health: the Health Research Committee, the Renal Dysplasia Information Committee, and the Gene-Mapping Committee. Among its various projects, the Health Research Committee has conducted a health survey of our breed and is preparing a booklet on breed-specific health problems. The Gene-Mapping Committee is involved in a research project to locate a genetic marker for renal dysplasia, a developmental defect of the kidneys found in our breed. If you would like to learn more about this disease, a free pamphlet on renal dysplasia is available from the ASTC. The ASTC also publishes a pamphlet entitled "Breeder Guidelines" describing what makes a responsible breeder and the obligations of the owners of stud dogs and brood bitches. This pamphlet also provides information about genetic testing for known problems in Shih Tzu.

The ASTC publishes a variety of other pamphlets, books, and videos as part of its educational mission. For serious students of the breed, the club publishes a series of Historical Record Books containing pedigrees and photos of Shih Tzu champions and records of top producers and specialty winners. The official club magazine, the *American Shih Tzu Club Bulletin,* is published quarterly. It is available free to members and by subscription to non-members. To educate new Shih Tzu owners, the ASTC publishes a 16-page booklet *Your Shih Tzu: Care and Training.* Several free educational pamphlets aimed at newcomers to our breed are also available. These can be obtained from the chairman of the ASTC Breeder Referral Service, who can also put you in touch with ASTC members in your area who can provide you with more information on our breed. The various ASTC informational materials are also used by club members who volunteer to educate the public at dog fairs and other such events. Among the various ASTC educational videotapes are videos of the 1995 Breeder Education Symposium on the Shih Tzu Standard, Shih Tzu Around the World, and Shih Tzu in Agility.

One of the primary concerns of the ASTC is the welfare of all Shih Tzu. We have endeavored to meet the challenge of homeless and/or abused Shih Tzu by forming a national welfare and rescue committee, with a network of ASTC members across the country willing to provide identification of and assistance to Shih Tzu in trouble. Many ASTC member local clubs also run their own rescue operations. The ASTC also strongly encourages the spay/neuter of all pet-quality Shih Tzu to avoid contributing to pet overpopulation.

To become a member of the ASTC, you must submit an application form signed by two ASTC members in good standing. Your sponsors must have known you for at least one year and observed your willingness to follow all criteria for membership and to subscribe to the purposes of the ASTC.

For more information about the ASTC or its programs, please contact your local Shih Tzu club, an ASTC member in your area, or the ASTC Corresponding Secretary, whose address is available from the American Kennel Club. You also can obtain information on the ASTC web site: http://www.akc.org/clubs/astc/index.htm/

The Local Shih Tzu Clubs in the United States

Chicagoland Shih Tzu Club, Inc.*
Golden Gate Shih Tzu Fanciers (Northern California)*
Greater Milwaukee Shih Tzu Club*
Kopper Valley Shih Tzu Club (Utah)*
Metropolitan Atlanta Shih Tzu Club
Metropolitan New York Shih Tzu Fanciers
Mount Hood Shih Tzu Club (Oregon)
Puget Sound Shih Tzu Fanciers (Washington)
Puritan Shih Tzu Club (New England)
Shih Tzu Club of Greater Houston*
Shih Tzu Club of Northern New Jersey, Inc.*
Shih Tzu Club of Southeastern Michigan*
Shih Tzu Fanciers of Central Florida, Inc.*
Shih Tzu Fanciers of Greater Baltimore, Inc.*
Shih Tzu Fanciers of Southern California*
Trinity Valley Shih Tzu Club (Texas)
Twin Cities Area Shih Tzu Club (Minneapolis area)*
*indicates ASTC member club

REGISTER OF MERIT SHIH TZU

To earn an ASTC Register of Merit award, a Shih Tzu dog must have sired six or more champions and a Shih Tzu bitch must have produced four or more champions. The owner of an Shih Tzu must be a member in good standing of the ASTC in the year the award is granted. Between 1969 and 1997, nearly 375 Shih Tzu had earned this coveted award.

Aa-Li Wang de Kleine Oosterling
Ch. Aagalynn's I'm A Dandy
Ch. Afshi's Gunther
Aga Lynn's Three Rum Collins
Aga Lynn's Water Chestnut
Ah So Lizzie Borden
Ch. Akitzu Alwright With Ista
Ch.Akitzu Istabon of Kecamo Bay
Ch. Akitzu Strawberry Bon Bon
Ch. Ali-Aj Holy Smoke O'Dragonfire
Ch. Ali-Aj Wildfire of R And R
Ch. Ambelon's Son of A Gunther
Ch. Anh Wei The Heirrogant Snob
Ch. August Moon's Aim For the Heart
Ch. August Moon's Full of Spunk
Am-Can. Ch. August Moon's Sugar Daddy
Avalon's Choo Moo
Bambu Tibetan Blossom CD
Barbara's Ming Tu
Ch. Barrington's Windsong of Choo Ling
Am-Can. Ch. Beedoc's Bangaway
Ch. Beedoc's Chueh Shih Mei Jen
Ch. Bei Jing O Nathan of Shansi
Bei Jing's Dynasty of Shansi
Ch. Bel Air Tigherson of Shang T'ou
Ch. Beswick's Double Your Pleasure
Am-Can. Ch. Beswick's Limited Edition
Ch. Billie's Follie Little Shaver
Ch. Billies Follie Rapid Shaver
Ch. Bilor's Elizabeth
Am-Int. Ch. Bjorneholm's Pif
Bon D'Art Ciao of Fancee
Ch. Bon D'Art Tu Tone of Fancee
Ch. Brownhill's Yolan of Greenmoss
Ch. Cabrand Agent Orange v Louwan
Cabrand's Ciara of Louwan
Camelot's Beau Brummel
Ch. Caralandra's Passing Fancy
Ch. Car-Lyn's Foxy Lady of Cambalu
Ch. Carrimount Ah Chop-Chop
Ch. Carrimount Ah-Crepe-De-Chine CDX
Cha Shu v d Oranje Manege CD

Ch. Chadomon's Guns N Roses
Am-Can. Ch. Chang Tangs Elusive Jeffrey
Char-Nick's Aliage of Shen Wah
Ch. Char-Nick's Executive Action
Ch. Char-Nick's I Gotcha
Ch. Char-Nick's Sesame of Sam Chu
Ch. Char-Nick's Studley Durite
Ch. Char-Nick's Swing Ehr of Copa
Charing Cross I Wanna Beastar
Ch. Charjalong's Bronze Bandit
Charjalong's Thai of Phildore
Ch. Chateau's White Peony of Arlys
China Chimes Jasmine N Jade
Ch. Chinai's Extra Special
Ch. Chinawood Jih-Lo
Ch. Ching Tsu of Marlen
Ching Yea of Lhakang CD
Chumulari Ch'ing Fu CD
Ch. Chumulari Chin Te
Ch. Chumulari Chin Te Jih
Ch. Chumulari Chung Hsia Te
Chumulari Hsia Chu CD
Chumulari Pao Shih
Chumulari Phola
Ch. Chumulari Ping Chu
Am-Can. Ch. Chumulari Sheng Li Che
Chumulari Trari
Am-Can. Ch. Chumulari Ying Ying
Ch. Concorde Crazy For You
Connemara's Fine Irish Lace
Ch. Copper Penny Dalai Fridlydid
Copper Penny Tas-Si
Ch. Dacun's Ah Sum Aramis
Ch. Dalai Delta Breeze
Ch. Dalai Hi Topaz
Ch. Dang Sai Angie Dickens
Ch. Dang Sai Little Jimi Dickens
Ch. Dashi's My My
Ch. Davanik's Classic Reflection
De Vilbiss Wind Song
Diandee Kee Mo No
Din Ho Wan Shih Poppy
Dominique Di Visconti
Ch. Don Wai Pardon My Dust
Donna Foo Young of Floridonna
Ch. Dragonfire's Adorable Dream
Dragonfire's Bonnie Blue
Dragonfire's Great Dracaena
Ch. Dragonfire's I'm Mahalia
Ch. Dragonfire's I'm No Lady
Ch. Dragonfire's O'Dashi
Ch. Dragonfire's Red Raider
Ch. Dragonfire's Shirley Ann

Ch. Dragonfire's The Great Draco
Am-Can. Ch. Dragonwyck Dominique
Ch. Dragonwyck of Charing Cross
Ch. Dragonwyck The Great Gatsby
Am-Can. Ch. Dun Kee Wang Socket Tu Ya
El Fran's Pardon Me Boys
El Frans Sparkle for M J
Ch. Emperor's First Lady Ch'eng
Ch. Emperor's Ping Pong Partner
Ch. Emperor's Top Line Designer
Ch. Emp's Cloisonne Glitter Ying
Encore Chopsticks
Ch. Encore Flower Child
Ch. Fancee Dari Heir of Bon D'Art
Ch. Fancee Heir Mhale Bon D'Art
Ch. Fashions J C Superstar
Ch. Forest Farm's Scheherazade
Ch. Foxfire No Assembly Required
Ch. Foxfire Winter Robin
Gardner's Black Devil
Ch. Garvin's Topaz of Runkel
Ch. Genisa's Miss Rosie O'Grady
Ch. Gensing's Incredible Chi Chi
Glaranik Amazing Grace
Glenka Tzi v Kleine Vossenburg CD
Golden Bobbin of Elfann CD
Ch. Granville Sno Dancin
Greenmoss Chin-Ki of Meo CD
Ch. Greenmoss Gilligan
Ch. Greenmoss Golden Talon of Elfann
Ch. Greenmoss Jezebel
Ch. Grenoville Hoodwink
Ch. Gunning's Better Half
Gunning's Hi Eye Cue
Ch. Gunning's Highway Robbery
Ch. Gunning It's a Wonder
Ch. Gunning's On The Make O'Loubren
Ch. Gunning's The Eighth Wonder
Ch. Gunning's Typografical Errer
Ch. Halcyon's Genie of Mei Shan
Ch. Halcyon's Sweet Dreams
Ch. Heatherwood's Hot Deal
Ch. Heavenly Dynasty's Olivia
Heavenly Dynasty's Wan Shi
Ch. Hee Shee's Wee Bell Ange
Ch. Hideaways Mei Ah Winemaker
Ch. Highland's Spice and Ice
Ch. Ho Chi Ring Leader
Ch. Hodari Lord of the Rings
Ch. Hodari Tam Lin of Moonling
Ch. Imperial Ping Tan
Ch. Imperial Pong Tan
Ch. Imua the Gatsby's Pride of Ali Aj CD

Ista's Can't Be Wrong
Ch. Ista's Wicked Fantasy
Am-Can. Ch. Jaisu Ling-Ho Chinese Junk
Jaisu Ling-Ho Pla-Toi O'Dynasty
Ch. Jaisu Ling-Ho X-Rated of Lainee
Am-Can. Ch. Janiric's Jumbo-Laya
Am-Can. Ch. Jazmin's Drummer Boi of Anh Wei
Ch. Jazmin's Maxi Million
Jazmin's Puff N' Stuff
Jazmin Such A Dickens
Ch. Jen Len's Magique Magpie
Ch. Jo-Ahn's Alexis O'Munchkintown
Ch. Jolei Chinese Checker
Ch. Jolei Jawbreaker
Ch. Jolei Lucille
Ch. Jolei Margarita
Ch. Jolei The Artful Dodger
Ch. Jolei Zsa Zsa
Ch. Joy Tu Ring of Fire Luken
Juling Miss Chief
Ch. Kachina's Sugar And Spice CD
Karyon Daphne's a Wonder
Ch. Karyon I'm Hot Stuff
Ch. Karyon Ming Dynasty Red Dragon
Ch. Karyon What A Dancing Man
Am-Can. Ch. Kee Lee's Munday's Child
Ch. Kee Lee's Red Baron of Mar Del
Ch. Ku Che Toi of Antartica CD
Ch. Lainee Sigmund Floyd
Ch. Lansu Magnolia Time
Ch. Lar-El's One In A Million
Li Ming's Bell-Bottoms
Ch. Li Ming's Carouser
Ch. Li Ming's Rebellione
Ch. Lilibet Golden Dawn
Ch. Long's Chiny-Chin Ah-Chop-Chop
Ch. Long's Kiko Lady
Ch. Long's Little Lick
Ch. Loubren's Annie's Song
Loubren's Blazin Annie
Ch. Loubren's Code of The West
Ch. Loubren's Dr. Mead
Loubren's Mistress of the Dark
Ch. Loubren's Ninja Star
Ch. Loubren Pippi Longstockings
Ch. Loubren's Saddle Tramp
Ch. Louwan Ambiance Crowd Rouser
Ch. Louwan Casinova
Louwan Casinovia
Louwan Forget-Me-Not
Ch. Louwan Kojak
Ch. Louwan Rebel Yell

Ch. Louwan's Rebel Rouser
Louwan's Red Lady
Louwan Scarlet Blaze
Am-Can. Ch. Louwan's Tootsie
Ch. Luken's All Fired Up
Ch. Lycobringarens Guy of Vitahund
Macada's Tribute to Char-Nick
Ch. Mah Jong's L'il Liza M
Ch. Mahal's Amadeus Mozart
Mandalay's Blockbuster
Mandalay's Ruf Tuf Creampuf
Ch. Mandarin's Royale Rhapsody
Ch. Mandarin's Sassy Samantha
Mandarin's Sweet N' Sassy
Ch. Mar-Del's Chow Mein
Ch. Mar-Del's Golden Sunset
Ch. Mar-Del's Moo Goo Gai Pan
Ch. Mar-Del's Ring-A-Ding-Ding
Ch. Mariljac Chatterbox
Mariljac Enchantress CD
Ch. Mariljac Kwang K'Whae
Ch. Mariljac Legend of Bomshu
Ch. Mariljac Marilyn of Chusanho
Ch. Mariljac Maripet
Ch. Mariljac Tinker Town Toi
Ch. Mei San Constant Comment
Ch. Mei San Jumpin Jack Flash
Ch. Mei San Peppermint Patty
Am-Can. Ch. Mei San Shindana
Ch. Mei Shan Stardust
Ch. Mejo's Kerri's Bear
Ch. Mijoy's Made My Day
Ch. Ming Dynasty Bamboo Shoot
Ch. Ming Dynasty Champagne Trade
Ch. Ming Dynasty's Chinese Sable
Ch. Ming Dynasty's Chinese Silk
Ch. Ming Dynasty's Dare Devil
Ch. Ming Dynasty's Dare To Dance
Ch. Ming Dynasty's Devil's Play
Ch. Ming Dynasty's Dragon Slayer
Ming Dynasty's Major Affair
Ch. Ming Dynasty New Star O' Bar-Lar
Ch. Ming Dynasty Shooting Star
Ch. Ming Dynasty's Silk Trader
Ch. Ming Dynasty's Tai-Phun O Re-Dan
Ch. Ming Dynasty's Wind Storm
Ch. Ming Toi Babbling Babs
Ch. Ming Toi P V Spunky
Miramar's Tapestry
Missy Mit Su Ling
Mistik Mylan Pao Kuei
Ch. Mo Tzu's Hellion of Toi
Ch. Monki Doodle of Midhill

Moon Ling's Tang Lee of Tien Tan
Munchkintown It's Me Lucy
Ch. Munchkintown Luv Me Doo Bubeck
Munchkintown's Busy Body
Ch. Munchkintown's Nevertheless
Munchkintown Street O'Desire
Ch. Mundy's Ama Yo Yo's Yum Yum
Ch. Mundy's Ama Yummer's Bummer
Can. Ch. Mystic Symarun Hugs & Kisses
Mytoy Dark Dancer At Beswick
Ch. Nanjo Hi-Hope of Joy-Fu-Li
Nanjo Ming Tiger Tue
Nanjo Miss Wiggles
Ch. Nanjo Oh Mai Gosh of Char-Nick
Nanjo Pien Tue
Ch. Nanjo Ping's Pat-Ti-Cake
Ch. Nanjo's Ah So Sweet Sum Wun
Ch. Nanjo's Wild Honey
Ch. Nanling Mi Merri Mimi
Can. Ch. Nan-Su's Dynamite Fantasy
Ch. Naysmith Jolei Jackpot
Ch. Ningsia's Fair Xchange Mei San
Ch. Nova's I'm No Pussover
Ch. Nova's Miss Dee Fying Min Dee
Org's Ama Rangers Tempest
Ch. Paisley Petronella
Ch. Paisley Ping Pong
Pako's Lotus Blossom
Ch. Parquins Pretty Boy Floyd
Ch. Parquins Sartezza
Peersun's Evening Ember CD
Pen San's Parti Crasher
Ch. Pen San's Eye of The Thai-Ger
Ch. Pen San's Koosa of Li Ming
Am-Can. Ch. Pen San's Parti Pet
Am-Can. Ch. Pen San's Parti Toi
Pen San's Parti Ying
Ch. Phildore's Woo-Fie-Do
Purple Jade's Penny Love
Ch. Red Raider's Cabbage Patch
Ch. R & R's Passionate Phillip
Ch. Regal's Dr Doolittle
Ch. Regal's Jack N' The Box
Ch. Regal's Kahlua and Cream
Regal's Properly Packaged
Regal's Su-Ze Q of Dorworth
Rockee Vollee Ailee Ali
Ch. Rockee Vollee Irish Red Bayley
Rockee Vollee Marzi Pan CD
Ch. Rojacky's Perfect Harmony
Ch. Rockee Vollee Velvetier
Rockee Vollee Victoria
Ch. Rojacky's Red Robin Fantasy

Ch. Rojacky Trade Off Ming Dynasty
Ronni's Amazing Grace
Ch. Sabar Snowfire of Marcliff
Saki Toome III
Sam Tsus Ta Shi
Am-Can. Ch. Sanchi's Vhima
San Yen Kan-Dee Kotton
Shaadar's Happi Boi Sam
Ch. Shado's Nickelodeon
Shali-Hi's Catch Me If You Cancan
Shali Hi's Melanie of Mei Shan
Shali Hi's Rainbow Raider
Ch. Shan Ku Kung Chu
Ch. Shang Ku Shang Ti of Bubeck
Ch. Shansi Domoni Bei Jing
Ch. Shar-Ming's Sweet Sumthin Spec'L
Sharn's Chantilly Lace
Sheik's I Hear a Symphony
Ch. Sheik's Luv-M-N-Leave-M
Ch. Shen Wah's For Members Only
Ch. Shen Wah's Turn It Loose
Am-Can. Ch. Shente's Brandy Alexander
Am-Can. Ch. Shente's Christian Dior
Ch. Shente's Jolei In Your Dreams
Shente's Manhattan Lady
Ch. Shente's Norma Jean
Ch. Shi-Seido's I'm Too Sexy
Ch. Sho-Lin Karola G'Day Mate
Ch. Show Off's Buckshot
Show Off's Catch of the Day
Ch. Show Off's I've Got Rhythm
Show Off's Marigold
Ch. Show Off's Minute Waltz
Ch. Show Off's Nobody's Perfect
Ch. Show Off's Visual Aid
Si-Kiang's Ester-Wu
Si-Kiang's Gumpy CD
Si-Kiang's Prci Phe
Ch. Snobhill's Free Lance CD
Ch. Sopon v Tschomo-Lungma
Soy Yo's Mannequin
Ch. Sparkle Plenty For David
Stony Lane's Imported Crystal
Ch. Stylistic Make Mine Cashmere
Ch. Stylistic Tiara Preference
Ch. Sukara's Take My Breath Away
Ch. Suki Mei Ling
Ch. Sun Canyon Hi Hopes
Am-Can. Ch. Symarun's Billy The Kid
T'ai T'ai of Shang T'Ou
Tai Shan's Guess Again

Taishan Tickle Your Fantasy
Talifu Fu-Hi CD
Ch. Tammashann's Ribbons of Fire
Taramount I Went Wong CD
Taylwag's Brandywine
Ch. Taylwag's P B R Donimie
Ch. Thompson's Tun Pu
Ch. Tiara Stylistic Twn-N-Country
Ch. Ti-Gi's Kiss of Dragonfire
Ch. Tipton's Lady Jen Mi
Ch. Toryglen Alpha Khan
Ch. Toryglen How Sweet It Is
Ch. Tu Chu Fire Opal Kimling
Ch. Tu Chu Golden Happiness Marja
Tu Chu Munchkintown Art Deco
Tu Chu Munchkintown Limitles'
Tu Chu Munchkintown Unlimit'D
Ch. Tu Chu Validian Desert Storm
Ch. Tu Chu's Mesmerized
Ch. Tu Chu's Reached the Limit
Am-Can. Ch. Tu Chu's Sky's the Limit
Ch. Tu Chu's Take It to the Limit
Ch. Tu Chu's You Only Live Twice
Ch. Tzi Tzi Shu
Ch. Validian Tu Chu Van Damme
Vilenzo Copper Penny Etc Etc
Ch. Vilenzo Hsing Ah Muk
Ch. Vilenzo Red Rover Red Rover
Am-Can. Ch. Wenrick's Chassen Rainbows
Wenshu's Lady An-Di
Am-Can. Ch. Willoway Stylistic SmakN'good
Ch. Willoway's Good Samaritan
Wingate's a Star Is Born
Wingate's Come Dance With Me
Ch. Wingate's Debutante
Wingate's Dust Ruffle
Wingate's Karyon Pollyanna
Ch. Wingate's Never Say Dye
Ch. Wingate's Never So Bubbli
Ch. Wingate's T K O
Ch. Wingate's Tom Terrific
Ch. Winward's Free Wheeling
Ch. Winward's Wheeler Dealer
Ch. Woodsmoke's Keep In Touch
Ch. Wychmiramar Sweet Baby James
Am-Can. Ch. Wyndee Cheerleader of Ho Chi
Yen Sing of Graywood CD
Am-Can. Ch. Yingsu's Johnie Reb
Can. Ch. Yingsu Lucky Lindy
Ch. Yosha Toddie Mikko Bear
Ch. Yoshi's Ah So Omar

Characteristics of the Shih Tzu

From its very earliest days, the Shih Tzu has been bred strictly as a companion dog. In the Chinese court, it was considered a status symbol to possess a dog that performed no useful function such as herding, tracking, or guarding. Although an occasional Shih Tzu might bark at a passing bird or butterfly, Shih Tzu in general are not "yappy" dogs. In fact, most rarely bark, although many of them express their wishes and moods via a very extensive vocabulary that includes yodeling, whimpering, and warbling. This means that if you want a watchdog, this breed is probably not right for you.

If, on the other hand, you want strictly a loving companion, the Shih Tzu may be the perfect dog. It wants nothing more than to love you. It is equally at home in a house in the country or a city apartment. Most Shih Tzu are anxious to play when you are (some, in fact, will bring you every toy in the house to encourage this), but when you are not at home they will sleep or amuse themselves.

Shih Tzu do not have great sex-related temperament differences. Males are just as affectionate as females, and easier to house train. Shih Tzu of either sex get along so well together that many people with one Shih Tzu decide to acquire a second one. Be careful, though, not to fall into the trap of thinking that if two are more fun than one, three or four will be even better. Do not let the fact that a Shih Tzu is not a demanding dog convince you that it thrives without human companionship. You want to be able to give each of your Shih Tzu the love and care it requires. Having a lot of Shih Tzu means that you will find it difficult and expensive to travel with them or find someone to care for them when you are on vacation.

If you do not like to groom a long-coated breed and are not willing to cut your Shih Tzu down into a pet clip, this is not the breed for you. Grooming a Shih Tzu requires a great deal of time and effort—and expertise, if you are to preserve the coat. Some coat textures are easier to care for than others, so ask for a pet with a sturdy coat if you do not plan to cut your dog down.

While Shih Tzu are classified as Toy dogs in the United States, they are not as small as most of the other Toy breeds. It is difficult to put a Shih Tzu into your purse and carry it with you. Even a small Shih Tzu is deceptively heavy for its size.

Shih Tzu have an almost human-childlike nature. They are sometimes described as "clownlike" or "catlike." They use their paws like hands when playing with their toys and will go to almost any extent to capture your attention. Their faces are so expressive that you could almost swear they are reacting to what you are saying.

While Shih Tzu generally get along well with children, be sure that your child is old enough (generally at least age five) to understand that a Toy dog is not a toy! ("That's Toy with a capital 'T', to you!") If not, you should wait a while before getting any dog. You must carefully supervise playtime with young children and your Shih Tzu to teach them to interact with each other in a safe manner. No dog likes being tripped over or having its tail pulled or its eyes poked at, and it can only defend itself by biting or running away.

Shih Tzu are intelligent and eager to please, but they can also be very strong willed. In a battle of the wills, your Shih Tzu can be very stubborn. Alternatively, it infuriatingly responds to corrections by kissing and tailwagging to try to convince you that you shouldn't

Shih Tzu have been pampered pets throughout their history, and the breed's personality reflects generations of being the "favored children." (Earl Takahashi)

have fussed at it. You need to be firm, consistent, and patient when training your Shih Tzu. It is often better to divert its attention or calm it down than shake it, scold it, or scream at it. None of these things lead to a healthy dog-owner relationship. At the same time, don't let your Shih Tzu charm you into letting it do anything it wants, or you will wind up with an ungroomed, ill-behaved urchin.

This is a breed that is easy to love—and easy to spoil. That's one reason, of course, that we Shih Tzu owners love our breed so much. Where else could you find so much affection in such a sturdy, attractive, intelligent, small package? If you decide, after reviewing the charactistics of the breed, that a Shih Tzu is the right dog for you, we're sure you'll never regret that decision.

Be sure your children are old enough to play safely with a small dog. This teenager blows bubbles for her Shih Tzu to catch. (Felicia Kelly)

Shih Tzu get along well with other dogs, large and small. (Phyllis Celmer)

Shih Tzu are hams; this therapy dog, dressed to kill, has been taught to beg. (Phyllis Celmer)

If you are not prepared to groom the breed's long, flowing coat, you may wish to give your pet an attractive clip. (Wayne Wright for Vicky M. Bloemer)

Shih Tzu come in all colors; they may be solid, parti-, or tri-color, although they normally are not found in solid white. (Sandra Martin)

Shih Tzu are smart as well as beautiful. Many enjoy participating in performance events such as obedience and agility. (Kathy's Portraits for Michael Shea-Zackin)

Choosing Your Shih Tzu

SELECTING A PET PUPPY

You have decided that you would like to become the proud parent of a Shih Tzu puppy. Congratulations! Few things in life are more satisfying than giving a good home to a loving and lovable puppy! But right now, before you fall in love with the first adorable Shih Tzu face you see, take the time to ask yourself some questions to be sure that you can offer a good home to a Shih Tzu puppy for the rest of its life. You may decide that this is not the time for you to get a dog, that the Shih Tzu is not the right breed for you, or that you would rather provide a home to an older Shih Tzu who needs one.

QUESTIONS TO ASK YOURSELF:

Are you prepared to take full responsibility for this dog and all its needs for the next 10–18 years? The training of and care of a Shih Tzu is *not* a task that can be left to children. It requires commitment from an adult.

Can you invest the considerable time, money, and patience it takes to train a dog to be a good companion? (This does not happen by itself!!!)

Will you keep your Shih Tzu as a house pet and exercise it on a leash or in a securely fenced yard and be sure it gets enough attention and exercise?

Are you willing to spend the money it takes to provide proper veterinary care, including, but certainly not limited to, vaccines, heartworm testing and preventative medication, spaying or neutering, and annual check-ups?

Will you take the time and effort to become educated about the proper care of the breed, correct training methods, and how to groom? The Shih Tzu is a long-coated breed and requires regular grooming. A severely matted Shih Tzu is uncomfortable and likely to develop skin problems. You must at least be responsible for daily maintenance. If you can't do it all, can you afford to take your Shih Tzu to a groomer regularly and/or be willing to keep it in a "puppy cut"?

Don't be afraid that you will sound foolish if you ask questions. You should be willing to take your questions to the breeder or other professional before they become problems that are out of hand. Most problems can be resolved easily if addressed in the early stages.

Puppies are a joy, but are you aware that they are also very time-consuming and need consistent, loving training? Adolescence can be a trial in canines as well as in humans, and older dogs often require special attention. Do you have the patience to deal with all of these stages in your Shih Tzu's life, and will you continue to accept responsibility for your Shih Tzu despite inevitable changes such as new babies, kids going off to school, moving, or returning to work? Dogs are not throw-aways! If you are not prepared to keep your puppy for the rest of its life, buy a goldfish!

If you answered yes to *all* of the above, you are ready to start contacting breeders. Start early because most responsible breeders have a waiting list ranging from a few months to several years. Resist impulse buying and have the patience to make a responsible choice. Remember, the right dog *is* worth waiting for!

All Shih Tzu puppies are cute, so keep the following checklist by the phone when you make your initial phone call to a breeder. You may not find a breeder who fits 100% of these criteria, but if you receive more than two negative responses, consider another breeder. Remember, your puppy will be a part of your family for many years.

Do not be in a hurry. If getting a Shih Tzu, any Shih Tzu, *right now* is foremost in your plans, then you are not serious and will get what you ask for…just any Shih Tzu. Now is also not the time to bargain hunt. The initial cost of your puppy, pro-rated over the life of the dog, is a very small part of the total cost of Shih Tzu

All Shih Tzu puppies are cute. Before you buy a Shih Tzu, learn enough about our breed to be sure it is right for you and be prepared to be a responsible dog owner. (Connie Warnock)

You may have known someone who has (or you may yourself have purchased) a "backyard" bred dog or a puppy mill dog and had great success. However, it is prudent to remember that such puppies may have health or temperament problems due to a lack of knowledge on the part of the breeder about breed health problems and genetics or a failure to provide proper socialization at a young age. Responsible breeders do all that they can to screen for and eliminate health and temperament problems. They also can provide you with advice about your puppy both before and after you take it home.

ownership. Saving a few dollars now will cost you a lot in the future. The better educated you are, the wiser selection you are likely to make. Read books on the breed, attend dog shows, and learn.

Finally, responsible breeders are expected to produce Shih Tzu to high standards. They are entitled to respect and courtesy from the people they are trying to please. Always be on time for any appointments and be honest in explaining your lifestyle, family activity level, experience with dogs, and knowledge of Shih Tzu.

Good luck in your search!

QUESTIONS TO ASK OF/ABOUT A BREEDER:

Where did you find out about this breeder? Responsible breeders usually breed only when they have a waiting list of buyers and don't need to advertise in newspapers or put a sign in the yard. You can obtain the name of a breeder in your area who is a member of the American Shih Tzu Club through the ASTC Breeder Referral Service. The telephone number for this individual is listed on the AKC Breeder Referral Representative Hotline (1-900-407-7877).

How often is the dam bred? Breeding every heat cycle is *too often* and may indicate that sufficient thought was not put into the breeding.

How long has the breeder been breeding Shih Tzu? Does the breeder trace health problems in the dogs he or she sells? If the breeder is new to the breed, has he or she carefully researched the genetic problems that may lurk in the background of his lines?

Will the breeder take the dog back at any time, for any reason, if you cannot keep it? This is the hallmark of responsible breeding (and the quickest, best way to make rescue obsolete).

Will the breeder be available for the life of the dog to answer any questions you might have? Is this someone you would feel com-

It is important that Shih Tzu puppies not be removed from their mother and littermates too early; they must learn to get along with other dogs as well as people. (Steve and Julie Schaull)

Shih Tzu come in many colors. Blue Shih Tzu have blue eyes and slate blue pigment. (James Hall)

fortable asking any type of question? If you feel intimidated or pressured, keep looking!

Is the breeder knowledgeable about the breed? Does he or she represent his dogs as honestly as possible and try to assist the serious novice in understanding the breed? Is he or she involved in competition with his dogs (conformation, obedience, agility)? Responsible breeders try to breed dogs as close as possible to the breed standard, which does not recognize "toy" or "imperial" Shih Tzu. Shih Tzu far below the normal weight range for the breed may have health problems. If you want a truly tiny dog, select another breed.

Are there a majority of titled dogs (the initials CH, CD, etc., before or after the names) in the first two generations? The term "champion lines" means nothing if those titles are back three or more generations or if there are only one or two in the whole pedigree.

Many companion Shih Tzu have their hair cut short, so that they are easier for their owners to care for. Shih Tzu in such clips look puppy-like throughout their lives. (Michael Shea-Zackin)

HOW TO READ A PEDIGREE

Your breeder should provide you with at least a three-generation pedigree, which describes the ancestry of your puppy. Remember that the further removed a name on the pedigree is from your puppy, the more distant its genetic relationship is. One or two champions among your puppy's great-grandparents have likely had very little influence on the quality of your puppy. Also, the number of champions in a pedigree per se is referred to as inbreeding (the breeding of father to daughter, mother to son, or full-brother to full-sister) or linebreeding (breeding to obtain the name of one certain dog on a pedigree as many times as possible). Inbreeding and linebreeding are ways to increase genetic uniformity. Their success depends upon the quality of the dogs used, because breeding closely related animals tends not only to fix desirable qualities but to bring faults that may have been masked to

A Shih Tzu in coat can quickly become a matted mess if it is neglected. Even if you use a groomer, you must still brush your dog regularly and clean its face. (Earl Takahashi)

less important than whether or not the champions found there tend to produce outstanding offspring. Conscientious breeders try to learn as much as possible about every dog found in the pedigrees of their breeding stock. In canine terminology, a male is referred to as a "dog" and a female is a "bitch." You will often see the same dog (or its brother or sister) repeated more than once in a pedigree. Depending upon the closeness of the relationship, such genetic doubling is the surface. In other words, one will generally obtain excellent puppies or terrible puppies. Outcrossing (the breeding of unrelated or distantly related animals) may produce offspring with hybrid vigor, but such offspring may or may not breed true because they often lack the genetic uniformity needed to fix a desirable trait. The pedigree that follows is an example of a total outcross, in which the same dog never appears more than once.

Dog G (great-grandsire)
Dog C (grandsire)
Bitch H (great-granddam)
Dog A (your puppy's sire or father)
Dog I (great-grandsire)
Bitch D (granddam)
Bitch J (great-granddam)
Your Puppy
Dog K (great-grandsire)
Dog E (grandsire)
Bitch L (great-granddam)
Bitch B (your puppy's dam or mother)
Dog M (great-grandsire)
Bitch F (granddam)
Bitch N (great-granddam)

The color in gold and gold and white Shih Tzu may range from pale cream to a deep, rich red. (Phyllis Schwab)

A grizzle Shih Tzu. (Sandra M. Whitten)

Are the puppy's sire and dam available for you to meet? If the sire is unavailable, can you call his owners or people who have his puppies to ask about temperament or health problems? Pictures or videos are especially helpful if you are purchasing a puppy from a breeder who does not live nearby.

Is the breeder knowledgeable about raising puppies, critical neonatal periods, and proper socialization techniques? Young puppies should not be raised in a pen in the back yard or live in isolation and should not be removed from their dam or littermates before eight weeks of age. (The ASTC Code of Ethics suggests puppies not be sold before 12 weeks.) The better socialized your puppy is when you receive it, the better the chances that it will grow up to be a well-adjusted adult.

Does the breeder provide a three- to five-generation pedigree, a complete health record, and material to help you with feeding, grooming, training, and housebreaking?

Does the breeder advise you to have the puppy checked promptly by a veterinarian and provide a written agreement to refund the purchase price or take the puppy back and replace it if it is found to be unfit by a veterinarian? While many dog sales are made without contracts, more and more reputable

Liver Shih Tzu, like blues, lack the gene for black. They have brown noses and eyes. (George Jones)

breeders are using written contracts. The reason is simple: such a legal document can resolve potential future problems between the buyer and seller. Generally, any contract should, at minimum, contain the names and addresses of the parties involved; identification of the breed of dog, birth date, and AKC registration name and number (or its AKC litter number or the AKC registration numbers of its sire and dam); the purchase price; and any guarantees provided by the breeder. The registration information is necessary for the AKC to be able to help you if you later have any problems registering your dog.

Has the puppy received the necessary immunizations and been checked for parasites and treated if necessary? Is the breeder knowledgeable about and working to control and/or eradicate conditions, including those that are particular to the breed, such as renal dysplasia, portal systemic shunt, hip and eye problems, allergies, von Willebrands disease, thyroid disorders, and inguinal hernias?

Have the puppies' temperaments been evaluated and can the breeder guide you to the puppy that will best suit your lifestyle? A very shy puppy will not do well in a noisy household with small children, just as a very dominant puppy won't flourish in a sedate senior citizen household. A caring breeder will know the puppies and be able to help you make a good match.

Do the puppies seem healthy, with no discharge from eyes or nose, no loose stools, no foul smelling ears? Are their coats soft, full, and clean? Do they have plenty of energy when awake yet calm down easily when gently stroked? If the puppy is in good weight, a slight, clear nasal discharge may be due to pinched nostrils, which are quite common in Shih Tzu puppies during the teething phase. Slightly pinched nostrils (those not severe enough to interfere with eating) generally open as the puppy matures. Small umbilical hernias, another problem commonly found in Shih Tzu puppies, almost always close with age, so do not be in any hurry to have surgery performed.

Does the breeder have only one or at most two breeds of dogs and only one litter at a time? If there are several breeds of dogs, the breeder may not devote the time it takes to become really knowledgeable about the breed. If there are several litters at a time, it is very difficult to give the puppies the attention they need and may indicate that the primary purpose for breeding is profit, rather than a sincere desire to sustain and improve the breed.

While not all responsible breeders are active in their national or local breed clubs,

A solid black Shih Tzu. (Robin Taylor)

such membership indicates a concern for the welfare and betterment of the Shih Tzu breed. Any ethical breeder, whether a club member or not, should follow standards similar to those in the ASTC Code of Ethics.

If there is a breeder whose dogs you like, you would probably be better off to put your name on a waiting list for a puppy than purchase from a lesser source just because the puppy is immediately available. Christmastime is *not* a good time to buy a dog, because you will not have the time needed to devote to introducing it to your household. Give a photo and dog supplies and introduce the puppy when things are calmer. If you are buying from a distant breeder, try to schedule

A gold and white Shih Tzu on the pale side of the spectrum.

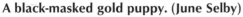

A black-masked gold puppy. (June Selby)

your puppy on a direct flight, even if it means traveling to a more distant airport.

PURCHASING A SHIH TZU FOR SHOW

All of the above comments about purchasing from a responsible breeder are even more important if you think you want to show your dog, because if you are a novice to the dog-show sport, your breeder is likely to become your mentor. The more knowledgeable the breeder, the more likely you are to acquire a quality puppy and the help you need to show it successfully.

You need to do your part, however. Attend as many dog shows as you can, read books about the breed and about training dogs for the show ring, and carefully study the Illustrated Guide to the Shih Tzu Standard. Understand the commitment in time and money required to show a dog and be sure that you are willing and able to undertake the task. The harder you have worked to learn about our breed—including structure, temperament, training, and coat care—the more likely a breeder will be to allow you to purchase a quality dog. Such dogs are few and far between, and nothing is more disappointing for a breeder than to sell a beautiful

A black and white Shih Tzu. (Phyllis Celmer)

dog to a novice exhibitor and have that dog never appear on the show scene.

After you have done a lot of studying of the breed, make it clear to the breeder just what matters to you in a show dog. Because the perfect Shih Tzu has never been born, list your priorities. What characteristics are most important to you, what flaws will you tolerate, and what faults are totally unacceptable. Ask about health problems; the introduction of unwanted health defects can ruin a breeding program. Some breeders do give guarantees on show stock, but they cannot be expected to be responsible for the fact that a dog did not finish because the buyer ruined its coat or otherwise rendered it unfit for the show ring.

If you want to purchase a young puppy as your prospective show dog, remember that many things can go wrong as the puppy matures. Almost every Shih Tzu puppy goes through the "adolescent uglies," when different parts of the dog develop at different rates. Some of these stages, such as the beagle-like tail carriage often seen in a puppy cutting its second teeth, may be only temporary. Others may be permanent.

A brindle and white Shih Tzu. (Kim Gropp)

These two Shih Tzu, at 9 and 16 pounds, are at the outer ideal weight limits of the breed standard. Very tiny Shih Tzu are not correct and may be small due to health problems.

When selecting a show puppy, become familiar enough with the breed to recognize obvious faults that will make a puppy unfit for the show ring. The puppy above left has the correct broad and round Shih Tzu head and straight front legs. The puppy above right has a low-set, down-tilted muzzle and will lack the proper expression. The puppy lower left lacks leg and neck, while the one lower right is high and straight in the rear. Such faults will not interfere with a puppy's health or ability to make you a fine companion.

If you purchase a young show prospect, it is very important to buy from a breeder who is very knowledgeable about how his lines develop. Even then, the breeder can only make an educated guess about a young puppy's potential. We all have tales of the promising puppy that later fell apart, and the ugly duckling sold to a pet home who matured into a spectacular specimen.

If you are buying your first show dog, you may be better off with a male, for several reasons. First, hormonal changes make it harder to keep a female in show coat. Also, a breeder is more likely to be willing to part with a quality male because he can keep only so many males from the same lines. Sex really doesn't matter in terms of companionship either. A male can be just as sweet and cuddly as a female, and is usually easier to housebreak. It is the personality of the individual dog that is most important, whether you are purchasing a show dog or a pet.

Remember, too, that not every show prospect completes its championship, and that very few of these champions become truly great dogs. For most of us, our first show dog was primarily a learning experience—the way we got our feet wet, paid our dues, made a lot of new friends, and learned how little we really knew.

These puppies are from a linebred litter, so it is understandable that they look very much alike (although they are clearly male and female).

You may prefer to purchase an older show dog because you know exactly what you are getting. The price will be higher because the breeder has put more time and money into the dog, but you are less likely to be disappointed.

If you think you want to show in either conformation or obedience and other performance events, or if you want to breed your dog, be sure to get a good specimen of the breed suited to your needs. Also, be sure that you will be able to register your dog with the AKC, and be sure to do so by the time the dog is one year old. If the breeder cannot provide the AKC registration application, you must receive full identification of your dog from the seller in writing—the breed, the AKC registration numbers of its sire and dam, its birth date, the name of the breeder, and (if available) the litter registration number. If the seller is unwilling to provide this information, which you *must* have to register your dog with AKC, do not buy the dog. Remember, however, that AKC registration per se does not mean show quality! It only certifies that your dog's parents and its litter have been recorded as purebred in the AKC Stud Book.

These littermates are from an outcrossed litter and bear little resemblance to one another. (Carlene Snyder)

Above: An exercise pen can create a secure outdoor play area for your Shih Tzu. Never let your dog to roam unsupervised; it may run off with a stranger or be hit by a car. (Sandra M. Whitten)

Right: Shih Tzu and Pugs are the largest of all Toy breeds. Sturdy despite its relatively small size, the Shih Tzu gets along well with children and other dogs of all shapes and sizes. (Earl Takahashi)

Shih Tzu are one of the few breeds that have hair instead of fur, which makes the breed suitable for people allergic to fur. (Joan McGee)

WHAT ABOUT AN OLDER SHIH TZU?

You might want to consider purchasing an older Shih Tzu as a pet or providing a home to an abandoned Shih Tzu that might otherwise have to be euthanized. Sometimes breeders have older dogs they would like to place in pet homes. These may be puppies kept for show that didn't quite "make the grade," or they might be retired champions or breeding animals who would appreciate spending their later years as pampered "only dogs" rather than as one of many. Because Shih Tzu are friendly, loving animals, they generally adapt well to a change of owners even later in life.

If you decide on a rescue dog, you might also save a life. Rescue dogs in need of loving homes may or may not have been responsibly bred. However, since they are adults, rescue workers are able to evaluate them for any signs of a problem *before* you fall in love, something that can't be done with a puppy. Rescue workers think this is only one of the advantages to adopting an older dog! The ASTC and many local Shih Tzu clubs run rescue operations; they typically ask for a donation to cover the veterinary care needed by rescue dogs and other expenses of running rescue programs. You may find that you wish to become involved in rescue work yourself. Volunteers are always needed.

Your Shih Tzu will be an active part of your family's life for many years. This Shih Tzu brought tears to everyone's eyes by winning the 1990 ASTC National Specialty from the Veteran Dog class when he was nearly 12 years old, the oldest dog in competition among more than 200 entries. (Dave Ashbey)

If you plan to show your dog, you may want to purchase an older dog rather than a very young puppy. (Earl Takahashi)

Providing a home to a rescue dog can be a very rewarding experience. This rescue dog has visited hundreds of inner-city school classrooms with his new owner, helping to teach children about the responsibilities of owning a pet. He is also a pet therapy dog. (Donna Bové)

Your Shih Tzu Puppy

Your new Shih Tzu will be part of your family for a very long time, so it is important to bring him up properly. You should receive from your breeder basic instructions about puppy care, feeding, and training; a copy of your dog's pedigree (its family tree); and a health record indicating what inoculations your puppy has had and whether and when it has been tested and (if necessary) treated for parasites. You should also receive your puppy's AKC registration papers. Many responsible breeders give papers only upon proof that your puppy has been spayed or neutered, or grant only AKC limited registration (meaning that the dog's offspring cannot be registered) to pet puppies. Your breeder can explain why such procedures are necessary to curb the production of unwanted dogs.

Before you actually bring your puppy home, buy whatever food and equipment it will need and lay in a supply of newspapers and unprinted newsprint (perhaps also a floor grate to avoid paper-shredding and wet feet) if you will be paper training your puppy.

Shih Tzu puppies love toys, especially crocheted yarn balls, soft latex and plush squeaky toys, and braided tug toys. Thick round white rawhide chips or small rawhide chew sticks are OK to use with a young teething puppy, but rawhide toys are a no-no for adult Shih Tzu. They get caught in the face furnishings and can choke your dog if he tries to eat them when they soften. *Never* give your Shih Tzu chicken, pork, or other soft bones, which could splinter and choke him.

HOUSEBREAKING

Hopefully, your puppy's breeder will have begun the housebreaking process before you ever bring your puppy home. Nevertheless, a young puppy has little control over its bladder and bowels and will need to become acquainted with the acceptable area for elimination in its new home. Many Shih Tzu owners paper train their dogs for life, or train them both to use papers and to go outdoors. This eliminates the need to take the dog outdoors when it is raining or snowing and provides an acceptable place for it to use in case of a sudden attack of diarrhea when the owner is not at home. In general, it is easier to train a male Shih Tzu to go outside than a female, because the male likes to mark its property.

If you decide to paper-train your puppy, even if only for a brief period, the initial paper-covered area should be relatively large. Gradually you can reduce this area to the size of an opened newspaper, covered with unprinted newsprint and/or a floor grate for cleanliness.

Whatever method you choose, be on the alert for actions signaling a need to eliminate—circling, excitedly sniffing a small area, or beginning to squat. Even if the puppy has started to urinate, pick it up and take it outside or put it on the paper immediately. Don't wait for an "accident" and then punish the puppy. It can't locate and open the door itself! Nor can it easily make the connection between an accident that took place some time ago and a belated correction. Also, don't expect a very young child to be responsible for seeing that it goes outside.

Giving your puppy plenty of toys will help to keep him from chewing on the furniture or other forbidden items; be sure to "puppy-proof" his living quarters. (Steve and Julie Schaull for Ed and Lynn Szewki)

Never allow the puppy to have the run of the house unless someone is watching it. It will take several weeks for it to become accustomed to its new home and learn where the door to the outside (or the paper) is. Also, even a "housebroken" puppy can have an accident if it gets too excited. It is very important to deodorize an area where the puppy has had an accident, so that the urine scent does not tempt him to make the same mistake again. (Both club soda and white vinegar are good deodorizers.)

It is even more important to avoid accidents in the first place as much as possible. Puppies seem to be attracted to things on the floor, which means it is a good idea to pick up throw rugs, etc., until the puppy is outdoors trained or able to discriminate between rugs and newspaper.

Many Shih Tzu are not completely reliable until they are about eight to ten months old, although there are always exceptions. Because Shih Tzu are so anxious to please, it is much more effective to praise the puppy when he eliminates in the appropriate spot than to correct him after he has had an accident. One day, when you are just about to give up hope, the light will finally dawn.

If you are outdoors training, the puppy should go outside even if it is raining—under a tree or a patio roof, etc.—you take the umbrella. If it is really bad weather try placing paper on the floor of the garage. If you take your puppy out for a walk as part of its housetraining, do not end the walk as soon as the puppy eliminates. It may then decide that the pleasure of the walk will end as soon as it has done its business and delay the act as long as possible. It is best to have the puppy eliminate first and then walk and play. Remember that, in general, your puppy will need to eliminate upon awakening, after meals, and after playtime. Be sure not to confine your puppy to his crate for such a long period of time that he is forced to eliminate there. This will negate one of the great benefits of crate training.

Small-size, quality dog biscuits make tasty treats to reward your Shih Tzu for good behavior. Do not feed table scraps or encourage your dog to beg at the table.

CRATING YOUR SHIH TZU

Your breeder will probably have accustomed your puppy to sleeping and eating in its crate. Crating is not cruel. The crate is the puppy's "den," a safe, quiet place to relax—at home or when traveling. If you can, put the crate in a spot out of traffic (although a puppy in its new home may miss its littermates and mother less if its crate is placed next to your bed at night). Playing a radio or a nearby television should help settle the puppy. Playing all kinds of different music accustoms the puppy to strange voices and sounds. It also helps cover up odd noises that might frighten the puppy when it is alone.

Do not rush to your dog every time it barks or cries in its crate; this simply reinforces unacceptable behavior. On the other hand, don't overuse the crate. A young puppy is very energetic. It needs your loving attention and time out of its den to play, or it will become wild and unruly.

Once the puppy is comfortable in the house and can tell you when it needs to go outside, it will probably be very happy sleeping in someone's room/bed, but crate training is still valuable if you are going to leave your dog alone for a long period of time, if you are traveling, or if you are going to the vet.

You may want to attach a guinea pig or rabbit water bottle to the crate to provide fresh water for your puppy. Many breeders use water bottles even for their adult Shih Tzu because Shih Tzu using a water bowl tend to drip water off their mustaches and beards all over their chests and the floor. To continue using a water bottle without keeping the crate set up, select a spot which will always be accessible to your puppy and install two screw eyes (from the hardware store) on which you can attach the wire water-bottle hanger. Alternatively, stands designed specifically to hold water bottles are available; these can be moved about. The spout of the water bottle should be high enough off the ground so that the puppy reaches up to drink. In show puppies, this encourages them to extend their necks, which is desirable for nice carriage in the show ring.

YOUR PUPPY'S DAILY ROUTINE

When your puppy wakes up in the morning, it must immediately be taken outside or to the papers to relieve itself. You can carry the puppy out, or tell it, "Outside!" and have it follow you. Give it time to find the "right" place and to empty its bladder and bowels. Praise it when it is done to reinforce the idea that the outdoors is the right place to get relief. Do not leave the puppy outside alone. It may wander off and not find its way back, or it may go into the street or into a neighbor's yard where another animal may attack it.

Breakfast (using the food recommended by the breeder on the schedule the puppy is used to) follows elimination, and then a one-hour playtime–supervised, of course. Usually the combination of food and exercise tires the puppy and it will want to take a nap. Put it in its crate in a quiet place for a couple of hours. When the puppy wakes up, or when it is convenient for you, take it outdoors again. It can then play safely in the house for several hours. You can lead break your puppy and take it for short walks, which get longer as it matures.

Dinner is served in the crate, followed by a two-hour nap. Then, another trip outdoors, followed by a couple of hours of playtime before bed. When bedtime is announced—"Bedtime"—the puppy should be encouraged to go into its crate by itself by giving it a dog biscuit or another treat. It will normally be eager to jump in.

Shih Tzu drink readily from a water bottle, which can be attached to a kitchen cabinet or a special stand. This avoids wet faces and messy dripping all over the floor.

Even a young Shih Tzu puppy needs a topknot as soon as his hair hides his eyes. Tying up the hair keeps it out of your dog's eyes and mouth and his food dish. (JoAnne J. Mazur)

FEEDING YOUR SHIH TZU

Puppies are growing rapidly and should be fed diets specially designed for youngsters. If you wish to change the puppy's food or feeding schedule, do so gradually so as not to upset his stomach. Note that the puppy will usually let you know if he is getting too much or not enough to eat. If he begins skipping one meal regularly, it is probably time to eliminate it. If he leaves food behind, you are probably feeding him too much. Feed only as much as he will consume promptly. Tempting a reluctant eater with special foods or table scraps will only make your Shih Tzu a picky eater. A premium-quality kibble fed once or twice a day, with perhaps a small bit of canned food for flavor, is sufficient for a grown dog. Using dry food also helps to keep the mustache clean and white. Whatever food you ultimately use should contain enough fat to promote healthy coat growth. Supplementation with extra vitamins when feeding a well-balanced diet is generally unnecessary except under special conditions. In fact, excess quantities of certain vitamins may make your puppy ill. Many breeders use coat supplements for problem coats, and brewer's yeast supplements may help to ward off fleas. Overfeeding contributes to many health problems—so don't. A fat Shih Tzu is not your goal.

CHEWING

You will notice that your puppy uses its teeth while playing, seeming to love to bite everyone and everything. Although it is cute in a puppy, this can become a bad habit. Be sure there are plenty of toys—Nylabones® and Gumabones®—around so that, when your puppy starts to bite, you can substitute one of these for the finger, chair rail, etc. Be especially certain to instruct children in the importance of this, since youngsters usually find the puppy's chewing very funny while it has tiny teeth but very scary when the teeth get larger. For a puppy that begins to bite too hard while playing, the command "no bite," coupled with snapping the fingernail of your index finger against its nose, can be very effective in stopping this behavior.

Once your Shih Tzu is trained, he can be allowed more freedom unsupervised. Shih Tzu love to sleep on the bed! (Nancy Henley)

If your puppy is reluctant to walk on a leash, it may help to have him follow another puppy or an older dog that is already lead-trained.

SEPARATION ANXIETY

If your dog is well behaved when you are present but barks, forgets its housetraining, chews on inappropriate objects, or otherwise misbehaves whenever you leave it home alone, he is suffering from what animal behaviorists call separation anxiety. This means, in other words, that the dog misses you. Unfortunately, destructive behavior is one of the few ways a dog can demonstrate its feelings. Punishing your dog for this behavior only increases its anxiety rather than solving the problem. One way to get your dog used to being alone is to begin with many short periods of separation and gradually build up the length of time your dog can remain alone without becoming anxious. To lessen the anxiety, do not fuss over the dog just before you leave or immediately upon your return. You may wish to provide it with special and very desirable toys used only when the dog will be alone. Crating your dog when you leave for brief periods of time may be a good technique to curb destructive behavior, but only after the dog has come to consider the crate his den and feels comfortable and secure there. The best thing to do is to accustom your puppy early on to being alone, so that he learns that separation is something he can live with.

STOOL EATING

Some Shih Tzu have a very strong attraction to this disgusting habit. Although changing your dog's diet may help, in Shih Tzu this generally has nothing to do with what your dog eats or how clean/dirty its environment is. If your puppy seems to be acquiring this habit, it is up to you to control it. When you take the puppy outdoors to relieve himself, watch him closely. The second the puppy is done with his bowel movement, tell him what a good dog he is and call him to you. If he shows any interest in the stool, sharply say "NO!" and he should leave it alone. Don't be surprised if he returns to the stool later. Tell him "NO!" again and take him inside. Smacking the puppy or rubbing his nose in the excrement will not help; in fact, your dog may be more likely to eat his stool to avoid dealing with your response to it. If you are consistent, the puppy may outgrow the interest. Males do not seem as prone to this behavior as females.

Veterinarians have medication you can give the dog. But most people find that when the medication is stopped, the habit returns. Be sure to keep the area the puppy uses as his toilet clean to avoid encouraging this habit. You can buy a "pooper scooper" at a pet store so that you will not have to handle the droppings or even bend over to pick them up!

Do not allow an unhousebroken puppy the run of the house; this is a privilege granted only with careful supervision after a trip outside. (Felicia Kelly)

FLEAS AND TICKS

Many Shih Tzu are very allergic to flea bites, which are the real reason for many cases of skin allergies attributed to the breed. If only one flea bites a sensitive dog, the dog will scratch and bite and pull its hair out trying to get to the flea.

Flea shampoos and powders and dips do not work by themselves, and many of them are so harsh that they irritate the skin and dry out the coat. They may even affect the health of the dog. Of course, you must keep the dog clean and brushed (fleas love to hide under mats on a dirty dog). Use only a mild pyrethrin-based flea shampoo, preferably one containing coat conditioners, and kill any stunned fleas you may encounter while blow-drying your dog. An apple cider vinegar and water rinse acidifies the skin and helps to ward off future infestations; you can also spray a mixture of half apple cider vinegar and half water on hot spots created by flea allergies to help dry them up. The newest topical flea products on the market, available from your veterinarian, spread over the skin without being absorbed into the bloodstream; one application between the shoulder blades lasts for a month. Washing your dog's bedding frequently also aids in flea control.

The most important thing you can do to control a flea infestation is to treat your entire house with a spray containing Precor, a hormone that prevents fleas from maturing. By using this product, even if a flea comes into the house and lays millions of eggs, they will not mature. This will also protect you from flea bites. Such treatments last a long time. You usually only have to spray or bomb twice a year except in areas where you scrub the floor. Such areas can be spot treated more frequently. Spray only the perimeter of the room, since this is where flea eggs settle. There are also nontoxic powders containing boric acid for use on rugs that many Shih Tzu breeders have found effective. These powders damage the outer coating of the flea and cause it to dehydrate and die. Remember that fleas spend most of their lives off the dog. Using such

While your Shih Tzu will love to join you out of doors, a trip into the leaves or briar patch can destroy months of coat care. This is basically an "inside" breed. (Portraits Now for Sandra Martin)

Your puppy should be taught to obey basic obedience commands such as "come," "sit," and "stay." You can also teach him cute tricks and how to pose for photos. (Phyllis Schwab)

products is much better than constantly exposing your dog to poisonous sprays, powders, and dips. You can also spray the perimeter of your yard (away from the areas your dog frequents) with an insecticide to reduce the flea population in your dog's immediate vicinity, although such products are not flea-specific and may also kill beneficial insects, birds, and fish.

If you live in an area where ticks are a problem, check your dog frequently for these disease-bearing parasites. This is especially important if you live in an area where Lyme disease is endemic.

Shih Tzu love to travel, especially if trained when young. It is safest to confine your traveler in a crate or use a doggie car harness, and *never* let your dog put its head out an open car window. (Connie Warnock)

TRAVELING WITH YOUR SHIH TZU

Trips away from home with your Shih Tzu require planning and preparation. We recommend taking your dog's food dish with a supply of food; a water bottle (filled with your household drinking water or distilled water to avoid stomach upsets from water changes); a leash; cleanup materials; grooming supplies; a doggie first-aid kit; and your veterinarian's phone number (in case of emergency). Remember, *never leave your Shih Tzu in a car with the windows up during warm weather* or in your car during periods of extreme cold. Your Shih Tzu will be happier and safer alone in a hotel room while you go out to dinner if he has been crate trained.

Whether you are at home or on the road, be sure to be a responsible dog owner. Pick up after your dog, leave your hotel room at least as clean as you found it, and do not allow your dog to bark incessantly. If you do not do these things, you may find your community restricting dog ownership or campgrounds or hotels banning dogs. Remind other dog owners to follow the same rules.

If you crate-train your Shih Tzu from puppyhood, he will view the crate as his den, a place to relax and spend quiet time. (Phyllis Celmer)

This cut-down pet Shih Tzu has his own coat for cold weather. A brisk daily walk around the block (or chase games around the house) provide sufficient exercise. (Felicia Kelley)

TATTOOS AND MICROCHIPS

You may want to have your dog tattooed or microchipped so that you can identify it more easily if it should ever be lost. More than 100,000 pets so identified have been enrolled in the AKC Companion Animal Recovery program, which accepts either form of identification. For more information about this program, contact the AKC at 800-252-7894. This program is not the same as AKC registration, so you must fill out a separate form.

This Shih Tzu, in his life jacket and securely fastened, is enjoying a boat ride. Remember that most Shih Tzu do not swim well; be careful around swimming pools. (Nancy Henley)

Grooming Your Pet Shih Tzu

Some time during the day, every day, your puppy needs to be brushed. When your Shih Tzu is small, brushing will take only a few minutes, but these few minutes are critical training for when the hair gets longer and the puppy gets bigger and a grooming session may take 30–40 minutes. People who complain that they have to send their Shih Tzu to a groomer because it is so hard to handle have neglected this training. Most puppies do not want to lie still, but they can be taught. You will need a quality pin brush with flexible pins and a comb with a combination of close-set and wide-set teeth. Later, you may want to add a soft slicker, which is used to loosen mats.

You will need to be responsible for daily upkeep even if you use a groomer to bathe and trim your pet. Who knows, if you learn how, you may prefer to do the whole job yourself. If not, be sure the groomer you use loves dogs and knows his/her job. Going to the groomer should be something the dog enjoys, not something it dreads, and it is much more likely to take pleasure in this outing if you have not allowed it to become a matted mess beforehand.

BRUSHING YOUR SHIH TZU

To teach your puppy to enjoy being groomed, wait until it has used up some of its energy playing, then take it on your lap and gently brush its head and back. Holding it against your chest/stomach, brush its underbelly and the insides of its legs. This will only take a few minutes, but if it is done every day it will accustom the puppy to the brush and to your holding it in position. It is important to make grooming a pleasant experience. *Never let a misbehaving dog determine when you will stop grooming, as this will only reinforce undesirable behavior.* However, Shih Tzu can be very stubborn. It is better to stop brushing for a moment and speak calmly to your dog than to upset him even further when he is squirming and screeching. Don't put him down on the floor and let him think he's won a battle, just quiet him down and groom a bit more before ending the session while he is still behaving. He needs to know that in grooming, as in other matters, you are the boss—but also that letting you be the boss is pleasant.

Eventually you will want to teach your puppy to lie on its side on a table as you brush it (a rubber bathmat topped by a towel will make your puppy feel secure on the table). This is the same procedure you would use to dry it with a hair dryer after a bath.

As your dog grows more hair, be sure to part the coat and brush in sections all the way down to the skin. Never brush your dog dry. Spray its coat lightly before brushing with a mixture of one teaspoon of conditioner to one pint of water. Do not just brush over the top of the mats. The key to having a well-groomed Shih Tzu is to brush it often enough so that large mats never have a chance to form. Because small mats pull against the skin until the dog scratches at them, they can quickly become large ones that are almost impossible for an unskilled owner to remove. Ask your breeder to demonstrate how to brush a Shih Tzu. You may wish, especially as you are learning, to go through the dog with a comb after brushing to be sure you have removed all of the mats. Check especially on the insides of the legs, in the armpits, and under the ears, all the places where mats are most likely to form.

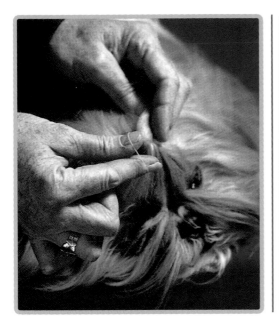

You should groom your Shih Tzu's face every day. When doing a topknot, you will be using a circle of hair extending from the bridge of the nose to outer corners of the eyes and around the top of the head. Once a dog has enough coat, doing the topknot in two sections (divided by a part straight across the center of the circle) will help keep the hair from falling forward into his eyes. First (above left), band the front half of the circle; put your bow on this section. Then (above right), band the back half; on both sections pull a small amount of banded hair toward the middle of the topknot tight to the scalp to hold the topknot securely. The two sections should then be banded together (below left), with the final band positioned below the band on the rear section and above the bow in the front section. Once the topknot is in place (below right), comb the mustache. You may want to use your knitting needle to pouf the hair in the front section (this will give your Shih Tzu a softer, more pleasing expression) and add a small dab of hair gel to keep stray hairs in place.

Train your dog to lie still for grooming from a very young age. Brush in layers from the stomach to the part, breaking up any mats with your fingers. When the brush reaches the end of the coat, lift it away to avoid breaking hair.

When brushing, always dampen the hair first. Leg hair should be brushed in layers toward the body.

If you find a mat, break it up with your fingers before brushing it out. This is less painful for the dog and causes him to lose less hair. You may also wish to make a teeth cleaning with a doggie toothbrush to prevent tartar buildup part of your daily grooming routine. Check your dog's eyes every day, removing excess matter, and see your vet promptly if you notice excess redness or tearing.

BATHING YOUR SHIH TZU

You may wash your puppy as often as it needs it—show dogs are usually bathed once a week. Dirty Shih Tzu not only are unsightly and uncomfortable but they mat more quickly. Before bathing your dog, brush and comb it thoroughly. Bathing "sets in" mats and makes them more difficult to remove. Sometimes only the face will need to be washed.

Among the basic grooming supplies are a pin brush with flexible pins, grooming and parting combs, a spray bottle (for your cream rinse and water pre-brushing spray), bows and latex topknot bands, scissors, guillotine nail clippers, a soft brush and cornstarch (for cleaning and drying the face), and perhaps a slicker brush, rake, or comb with rotating teeth (all useful in removing mats).

When giving a full bath, it is best to bathe your dog in a laundry tub or the kitchen sink (if it is large enough). Use a spray hose attachment on the faucet. This will give you more control over the dog and the flow of the water. Using a hair trap like those used in beauty parlors will keep the hair from clogging the drainpipe. Put a rubber mat in the sink so the dog will have firm footing, and dilute the shampoo with warm water before pouring it over the dog. Use straight tearless shampoo when cleaning the face. Be sure to shampoo and rinse the dog twice; the first shampooing doesn't really get the dog clean. Then pour a solution of cream rinse and water (your breeder can recommend suitable shampoos and conditioners) over the dog, avoiding the face. Leave some of the cream rinse in the coat for conditioning, rinsing until the coat feels only slightly slippery. Then squeeze out the excess moisture.

Bathe your thoroughly dematted dog in a sink with a spray attachment. Use a rubber mat for firm footing and rinse thoroughly. (Michael Shea-Zackin)

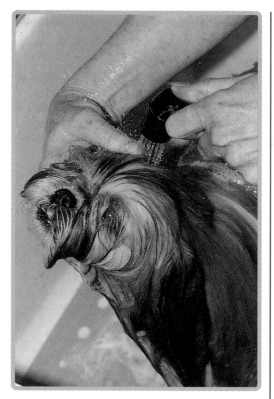

Blot away even more moisture by wrapping the puppy in a thick bath towel for a few minutes to speed drying time. Blow dry the puppy with a hair dryer (one on a stand works best because it leaves both hands free for the dog) while you brush the hair. The cream rinse and brushing while drying will give your pet the "show dog look."

BETWEEN BATH CLEANUPS

In between baths, if the face gets wet or looks dirty, or if little girls have stringy/smelly bottoms, you can use corn starch and/or corn-starch baby powder to freshen them. Corn starch is very effective on the mustache. It absorbs moisture and whitens at the same time. Just be careful not to get it in the puppy's eyes. Corn-starch baby powder is very good for little girls' bottoms. It will dry the hair and mask the urine odor between baths. There are occasionally little boys who might also benefit from baby powder underneath. When this remedy does not seem like enough and giving a full bath is impossible, use a self-rinse shampoo. These are available at pet stores and are easy to

Avoid getting water in the nose or ears when wetting and rinsing your patient Shih Tzu.

After removing excess moisture by wrapping your dog in a towel, use a dryer and brush the coat dry, again working in layers. Be sure the dryer is not set on high.

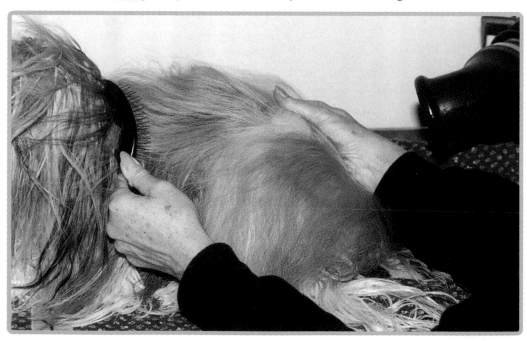

use. You can either saturate a cotton ball and "wash" the area needing cleansing (e.g., the mustache) or you can apply it directly from the bottle. Absorb the excess shampoo with as many paper towels as necessary and finish with corn starch or baby powder to "dry" the area. Some Shih Tzu have chronically wet faces that have an offensive odor, and self-rinsing their faces daily really helps.

If the "horror of horrors" occurs and your puppy returns from his outdoor exercise with his rear covered with poop, don't despair. The best solution is to put the offending area under running water. In an emergency, you might try standing the dog on newspapers (lots of them) and thoroughly saturating the area with baby powder. Brush or comb until the mess is gone. You may have to use several applications of powder to be successful. As the debris falls, wrap up the top layer of newspaper and put it aside so the dog can't step in it. When you are finished, the dog will smell and look better, and you can deposit the entire mess in the trash can. Be sure to check your dog's rear often, especially if you see it scooting its backside along the floor, as fecal matter impacted in the hair over the anus can cause a nasty infection and keep the dog from eliminating.

Topknot bows come in all sizes and colors to suit your dog's age, color, and head type. You can buy such bows or make your own. Latex topknot bands cause less breakage than regular ones. (Joyce DeVoll and Bonnie LaBarbera)

Use a knitting needle or a comb with a needle to part the hair along the spine. Then brush the hair to prepare the dog for trimming.

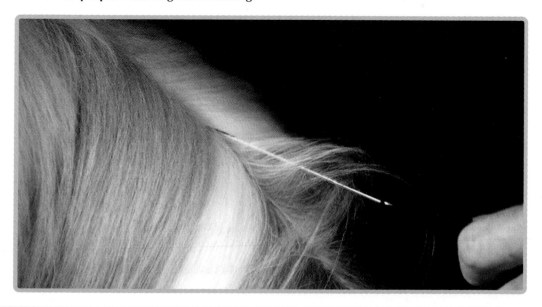

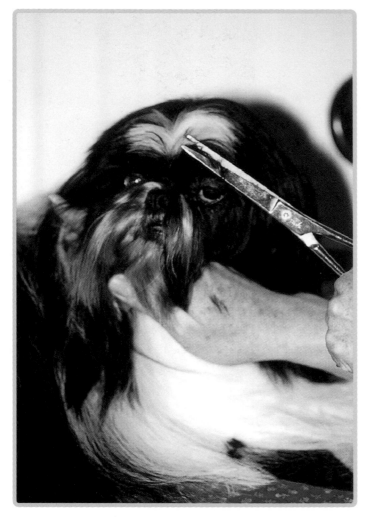

something coming at its eyes, this should solve the problem. Once the beard becomes long enough, you can control your Shih Tzu's head while grooming his face by grasping it by the chin whiskers.

Shih Tzu are prone to eye ulcers caused by objects such as hair clippings, grass, seeds, etc., getting into the eyes or by sharp objects scratching the eyes. These ulcers are very painful and can lead to blindness. *Such eye ulcers, which should be suspected when the dog tears excessively, squints, and has reddened eye whites, require immediate veterinary attention.* When you are combing the mustache, check the eyes. You can clean the eyes daily with any sterile eyewash designed for humans (look in the contact lens area of your local store). This not only will ensure that no foreign object remains in the eye to irritate it but it will also aid in removing the sticky gunk that accumulates in the corners of the eyes daily.

Even if you cut your Shih Tzu's topknot, it is helpful to leave enough mustache hair to hang onto to control your dog during grooming. This also eliminates short hairs over the bridge of the nose, which can irritate your dog's eyes

FACE AND EAR CARE

It is especially important to comb the mustache away from the eyes *every day*. Eventually the hair will be long enough to tie up in a topknot, and the hair on the bridge of the nose will lay down as a proper mustache should. Be very careful when using the brush or comb around the face so that you do not injure your puppy's eyes. If he seems to be afraid of the comb or shies away when you try to comb the mustache, try coming at the face from the chin. If the puppy was trying to avoid

Unless you have totally neglected your dog until there is no alternative, we recommend that you *do not* allow your vet or your groomer to cut the hair between the eyes or on the bridge of the nose. Once this hair is cut it must be kept clipped on a regular basis or the short hairs will get into the eyes and cause irritation. It is much easier to let the hair get long and comb it away from the eyes. There are many unfortunate stories about a puppy moving when its hair was being clipped and its eye was jabbed with the scissors, or about hair clippings lodging in the eye and causing an ulcer.

Besides brushing the coat and keeping the mustache in place, you also need to take care of the ears. Many breeders regularly remove excess hair from the ear canal. You can pull the hairs out with your fingers quite easily, especially if you use an ear powder. This will help prevent ear mites and yeast infections in the ear canal. If your dog has a foul-smelling or dark discharge from his ears, or is constantly shaking his head or pawing at his ears, take him to your veterinarian so that the problem can be diagnosed and treated. Neglected ear infections can lead to deafness.

FOOT AND NAIL CARE

The hair between the pads of the feet needs to be kept clipped short on a regular basis. Please use care (and a pair of blunt-end scissors) when trimming between the pads to avoid injuring your Shih Tzu. If your puppy has a very thick coat, you may find it necessary to trim the feet every couple of weeks. Also, trim the hair around the outside of the foot level with the ground for a neater appearance.

Nails need to be clipped at least monthly. This way you only have to trim a little and you don't have to worry about hurting the puppy. To trim the pads or clip the nails, hold the puppy on your lap with its back against you. Trim the hair first so none will be caught in the nail clippers. Then clip off the "hook" of each nail, and don't forget the dewclaw, which is the equivalent of the dog's thumb. If your dog has clear nails, you can see where the pink vein in the nail is; use this to judge how much to cut from black nails. You do not want to cut into this pink strip (the quick), as it will hurt the puppy and the nail will bleed. Keep a styptic handy when cutting nails in case you accidentally cut too far. If you are worried about taking too much, just clip the tip of the nail. A little is better than none at all. On a grown dog, it is easiest to cut the nails right after a bath, as they are softer when wet.

Using a guillotine clipper, trim the nails to where they hook over. On light-colored nails, you will be able to see the pink quick, which will bleed if you cut too far. It is easiest to cut the nails during the bathing process, because they are softer when wet.

Trim the hair around the anus. This will help to keep feces from clinging to the hair.

THE ANAL AREA

Have your breeder or your veterinarian show you how to express your dog's anal glands. The time to do this is just before a bath, because the anal gland discharge is extremely odorous. If the anal glands (which feel like small peas on either side of the anus) are not expressed regularly, they could become impacted and ulcerate.

One last place to trim is around the anus, just beneath the tail. Trim the hair at least one inch away from the opening and about an inch up the tail. Keeping this area clear of hair will mean a cleaner bottom if the puppy gets a runny stool from eating something it shouldn't.

THE SHIH TZU "COAT CHANGE"

Virtually every Shih Tzu "blows" its puppy undercoat at some time between eight months and one year of age. During this stage, the dog seems to mat almost as fast as you brush it. Some Shih Tzu coat changes are easier than others because the dogs blow coat in different areas at different times. This stretches out the process but reduces the daily work involved. Other dogs blow all of their undercoat at once and may need to be groomed several times a day to avoid stressing out both you and your dog. A heavily coated puppy may lose what seems to be a shopping bag full of hair in a week or two. It is at this stage that many pet owners throw up their hands in frustration and cut down their Shih Tzu. *Do not despair!* This is a one-time occurrence. Once the puppy undercoat is finally all brushed out, the adult coat is much easier to care for. During this stage, be sure to leave more cream rinse in the coat than normal to make it easier to remove the mats.

Round the feet and trim the side coat level with the table for neatness. Also trim the hair between the footpads or your dog will develop painful mats between the pads.

When you have finished bathing and trimming your dog, he will not only look good, he will also feel good. Grooming is not a task that can be neglected.

CUTTING DOWN YOUR PET

Many pet owners find it easier to keep their Shih Tzu in short haircuts to reduce the amount of grooming needed. There are many cute haircuts, such as the puppy, cocker, and schnauzer clips. Experiment until you find the cut best suited to your dog.

If you are going to attempt this yourself, you will need a good pair of electric dog clippers, a slicker brush, a comb, and scissors. Be sure to have someone knowledgeable demonstrate how to use the equipment before you try it yourself, as a too-hot blade or improper clipping techniques can cause severe burns or cuts. Cut with the growth of the hair to avoid burning your dog's skin, and be sure to cut down only a clean, dry dog.

Whether you decide to keep your Shih Tzu "in coat" or cut it down, we hope that the information in this book will make it much easier for you to care for your pet. If you are still having any problems, contact your breeder or an ASTC member in your area for a "hands-on" grooming demonstration.

You might want to simply scissor most of the hair short so that your adult Shih Tzu still looks like a puppy. Some breeders clip the body hair short but scissor the hair on the head and legs and leave the tail untouched for a more "finished" look. (Earl Takahashi)

Comfortable pet clips for your Shih Tzu. (Tammarie Larson)

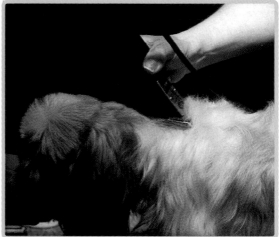

Many pet owners find it simpler to cut down their Shih Tzu to make grooming easier. This is much better than having a matted dog, and there are many cute cuts. This Shih Tzu (above left) is bathed and ready for a haircut. The groomer uses a #5 clipper blade (above right) on the back, clipping in the direction the hair grows to avoid burning or cutting the skin. A #7 blade (middle) is used to cut away the hair under the ears and at the outer edge of the eye to avoid mats and tearstains. After a final scissoring of the rest of the coat (bottom), the haircut is finished.

Pet Grooming Styles for the Shih Tzu

by Kandice Jones

Most pet Shih Tzu owners do not have the time or patience to keep their dogs in full-length show coat. Groomers trained in grooming classical styles for various breeds many times have had little training in how to do creative haircuts for our special dogs. In addition, most Shih Tzu owners have not seen a variety of haircuts complimentary to different Shih Tzu coats and body styles. Trying to find the right pet clip for your dog can therefore be very difficult. We hope that Shih Tzu owners and groomers alike will benefit from these descriptions of hair styles for our breed.

There are several variables to consider when deciding on a clip for the Shih Tzu. Most people are concerned about how much time a particular style will require in terms of home grooming and about their dog's comfort. Other important things to consider when choosing a hairstyle for your Shih Tzu are your dog's individual coat texture and body style, other breed-specific faults and characteristics, and your climate. What looks appealing to you as a Shih Tzu owner is also very important. After all, you are the one who has to live with your dogs. Most people want their dogs to retain some of the "Shih Tzu look" even when clipped in a pet style.

It is recommended that your dog be clipped at least every six to eight weeks to maintain these styles. Your groomer should also take care of ear cleaning and nail clipping when your dog comes in for a styling. Groomers are also used to checking for external parasites and skin problems that you may not notice yourself. Grooming is very hard work and requires a good eye, a steady hand, a ton of patience and dog savvy, and a lot of training. When you find a good groomer, be sure to let him or her know when you are pleased with the service you receive.

There are four different areas that can be varied in your pet's hair style. These are the body style, the head style, and, less importantly, the feet and tail styles. It is generally preferred to have some "balance" to the clip—fuller head, tail, and feet clips with fuller body styles and vice versa. The different styles—with instructions for and the advantages and problems of each—are described below. For *all* styles, it is assumed that the groin area, rectal area, and foot pads will be trimmed with a #10 or #15 blade.

*1. This is a **puppy cut**. It is shown with a full, rounded head style, cylindrical legs, and a full tail.*

Instructions:

Hand scissor the entire dog 1–3" in length perpendicular to the dog's body and legs, using straight shears. Thin undercoat in the appropriate areas to help the dog's legs appear perpendicular to the ground when viewing it from the front or rear. If the dog is heavy-bodied, thin the side coat to give it a thinner appearance.

Advantages:
* *The "puppy look" is very cute*
* *Most structural faults will be hidden*
* *The cut is warm in winter*

Disadvantages:
* *Most Shih Tzu in this cut need brushing at least twice a week, depending upon how quickly the coat mats*
* *This cut does not look well on flat or thin-coated dogs*

• This cut will not work well with coats that mat easily or are cottony or wiry in texture

• The dog may be too warm in extreme summer heat

2. The **schnauzer cut,** shown with a medium beard, a short topknot, cylindrical legs, and a tassled tail.

Instructions:

Using a #15, #10, #8.5, #7, or #5 blade, clipper the dog from the back of the skull downward with the growth of the hair (down and back towards the tail). Clip down to near the bottom of the rib cage and two-thirds of the way down the back bend of the upper rear legs. Clip the insides of the back legs to match the outside lines. Scissor the hair on the forechest and underchest and the side coat fairly short (about 1-2"). Leave about the same length on the leg furnishings. Use thinning shears to blend the topcoat where the clippered line meets the scissored line and underneath where the furnishings start to fall to create a more natural short-to-long look rather than leaving the hard clipper line.

Advantages:

• Easy to care for, as the dog requires less brushing and is quicker to bathe and dry than one in a puppy clip

• Easier to treat external parasites (fleas and ticks)

• Can be used on most coat types

• Is cool for most dogs in the summer

• Accentuates good rear angulation and topline

Disadvantages:

• Does not look good on dogs with poor toplines or straight stifles

• May be too short for some dogs in winter

3. **Short-bodied clip,** shown with medium beard, flagged tail, short topknot, and belled ears and legs.

Instructions:

Using a #15, #10, #8.5, #7, #5, or #4 blade, clip the entire body and chest, going with the lay of hair as above. Scissor legs 1–2" long and blend well, using the same method suggested in the schnauzer clip.

Advantages:

• Easy to care for in comparison to either of the two clips above

• Easy to treat external parasites

• Can be used on most coat types

• Cool for most dogs in summer

• Accentuates a good topline

• Makes dogs appear a bit more leggy and less long in body

• Good for heavy-bodied dogs

Disadvantages:

• Does not look good on dogs with poor toplines

• May be too short for some dogs in winter

• Requires an easy-care, low-matting coat texture

4. **Cocker style,** shown with medium beard, medium rounder ears, flagged tail, and tapered legs.

Instructions:

Using a #15, #10, #8.5, #7, or #5 blade, clip the dog from the base of the skull down and back to a line that runs horizontally about one-third of the way down the dog's body, or to about the point where the shoulder and upper arm meet. Scissor the chest furnishings longer than in the schnauzer style (about 4–5" in length). Blend in the furnishings as in the schnauzer clip.

5. **Full-furnishings clip,** shown with full beard, pig-tailed topknot, and full tail.

Instructions:

Clip neck and back as in cocker style. Blend in furnishings as in cocker clip, leaving sidecoat and legs at full length. If hair extends below and beyond the bottoms of the footpads, trim it even with the table top with scissors.

Advantages:

• Captures the look closest to the natural, unclipped Shih Tzu coat style
  • Is warm in winter
  • Accentuates a good topline
  • Looks good on most body types
  • Hides structural faults in legs

Disadvantages:

• High maintenance, requiring daily brushing and taking longer to bathe and dry than most other styles

• Rear coat on females and coat around groin and inner leg area on males may need daily washing to prevent urine and odor build-up

• Suitable only for dogs with low-matting coat textures

• May be too hot for many dogs during summer

• Coat will tend to pick up yard debris if the dog is not exercised on gravel or concrete

Advantages:

• Easier to care for than the puppy clip
• Good all-season clip
• Accentuates a good topline
• Good to create a more balanced look on long-legged dogs

Disadvantages:

• Does not look good on dogs with poor toplines or dogs that are long in body or low on leg

• May be too short for some dogs in winter

• Requires an easy care, low-matting coat texture

Head Styles:

Note: In general, cutting the hair short across the bridge of the nose and under the eyes is not recommended. It is very easy to injure the dog's eyes while cutting this hair. As the cut hairs grow in, they tend to rub against and irritate the eyes. Also, the owner has nothing to hold onto while cleaning and combing his dog's face and eyes.

1. **Puppy style,** with rounded look. Scissor topknot to about 1–2" all over. Leave beard about 3–6" long. Trim ears to blend in with beard to create a rounded look.

6. **Kennel clip,** with clipped ears, tassled tail, and rounded feet.

Instructions:

Use a #7, #4, or #5 blade (or a #30 with plastic clip-on attachment) everywhere except end of tail and a tuft over the foreskull. Scissor short over the nose in front of the eyes and shape the hair over the topskull to give it a dome-like appearance. Trim the edges of the ears and feet to a rounded shape.

Advantages:

• Easiest style to maintain, requiring little brushing and less frequent baths
• Very cool in hot weather
• The feet and face stay much cleaner
• Easy to spot skin problems and external parasites
• For dogs that like to swim, there is less hair to weigh down in the water
• Easiest and fastest clip to do if you do your own grooming

Disadvantages:

• Will show all of your dog's structural faults
• May look especially unattractive on dogs with very heavy bodies, long backs, or short legs

2. **Kennel style.** Shave all but a little hair over the foreskull. The remaining hair should be scissored to a tuft similar to a Cocker Spaniel. Trim short with scissors in front of the eyes. Round off the ears to blend in with the face, again trying to achieve a full, round look. A variation on this style is to leave the hair on the ears from about one-third of the way down on the ear, rounding off the ends as in a Cocker ear. While the hair on the muzzle is often removed in this style, we recommend not trimming the hair on the bridge of the nose or under the eyes to avoid eye injury or irritation.

Feet and Leg Styles:

*3. **Medium topknot with long beard.** Scissor topknot to about 1" in length from eyes to tops of ears to back of skull. Scissor bottom of beard and ears to blend in together, but leave longer than in puppy style.*

*1. **Poodle foot.** Trim just like a poodle, using a #10 or #15 blade to clean the feet and trimming the pastern and hock hair even with the top of the feet. For people who like full legs but don't like the trash and wet that the full feet bring in.*

*2. **Cylindrical leg.** The hair is trimmed to create a straight look from the lower part of the leg to the floor. As a variation on this style, for a bit cleaner feet, you can lift up the lower leg hair and shave the toes fully and trim a short way up the heel of the foot, letting the longer hair drape over the top of the feet.*

*4. **Pig-tailed topknot.** Part the topknot down the middle of the skull. Gather each side over the ear into small orthodontic bands or special latex Shih Tzu topknot bands and add bows. Again, scissor the beard and ears proportionately.*

*3. **Tapered leg.** The hair is scissored shorter closer in toward the feet. This helps to keep the feet somewhat cleaner.*

4. **Belled leg.** *Let the hair flare out at the feet. As a more practical variation, lift up the lower leg hair, shave the toes fully, and trim a short way up the heel of the foot, letting the longer hair drape over the top of the foot.*

2. **Flagged tail.** *Shave about 1–2" around the base of the tail, scissoring the rest of the tail hair to about 1–3" in length.*

Tail Styles:

3. **Tassled tail.** *Shave the tail almost all the way up with the same blade used on the body, or a little shorter one. Scissor the hair at the tip of the tail 1–3" in length. This look is reminiscent of the Oriental "lion dog" that figures so prominently in the breed's history.*

1. **Full tail.** *Leave the tail natural.*

In conclusion, have fun trying various styles on your beloved Shih Tzu. Be creative, but always keep your dog's comfort in mind and remember that all styles will not look good on all dogs. Your groomer should be willing to help you decide which style is best for both you and your dog. If you don't like the first style you try, just let the hair grow back and keep trying until you find just the right clip.

The Shih Tzu in the Conformation Ring

A dog show is like a giant elimination contest leading, ultimately, to a single dog being named Best in Show. There are several kinds of dog shows, ranging from fun matches and sanctioned matches, at which no AKC championship points are awarded, to AKC licensed dog shows, where your Shih Tzu can compete for its AKC championship and higher honors. These shows may be for all breeds, for a single breed, or for one of the seven groups (the Shih Tzu is classified in the Toy Group).

. Your Shih Tzu will be judged upon how well, on that day in that judge's opinion, it conforms to the perfect Shih Tzu as described in the Shih Tzu breed standard (although the dog's attitude and grooming and your handling skills do enter into the picture). Match shows are generally much less formal than point shows and are a good place to practice if you and your Shih Tzu are just beginning to learn the ropes. Ask your breeder or other exhibitors in your area how you can find out when and where such match shows are being held.

In examining the individual Shih Tzu, the judge will first take an overall look at the class and then examine each dog individually, both standing still ("stacked") and moving, before coming to a final decision about how well each dog in the class exemplifies the picture of breed perfection described in the breed standard. Both overall balance and soundness and breed type are important factors in making this decision. Because no dog is perfect, the views of the particular judge about which points in the standard are most important enter into the decision. This factor, plus the quality of the competition and how well a dog shows on a particular day, help to explain why a certain Shih Tzu may win one day and lose the next.

HOW A DOG SHOW WORKS

To earn an AKC championship, a Shih Tzu must earn 15 points under at least 3 different judges, including 2 major wins (wins of 3 points or more). No more than five points can be won in a single show. Only one male Shih Tzu (dog) and one female Shih Tzu (bitch) can win championship points in any one show. The number of points awarded is based upon the number of dogs of that sex in competition, as determined by the AKC schedule of points for the part of the country in which the show is held. This point schedule is revised each year based upon the number of dogs competing in the previous year in that area, so that a championship will always be difficult to earn.

Shih Tzu competing for their championships are entered in any one of six regular classes, divided by sex: puppy (which may be divided by age into 6–9 month and 9–12 month puppy classes), 12–18 month, novice (for dogs that have never won a blue ribbon for first place in any other classes or three first-place ribbons in the novice class), bred by exhibitor, American-bred (born in the United States from a mating that took place in the United States), and open (for any Shih Tzu). The dogs that win first place in each of these classes return to the ring to compete for Winners Dog (best male) and Winners Bitch (best female). These two winners receive the championship points for that day. The judge also selects a Reserve Winners Dog and a Reserve Winners Bitch (known to exhibitors as "best of the losers") as back-ups in case there was some mistake made in an entry that would disqualify the Winners Dog or Winners Bitch.

The Winners Dog and Winners Bitch then compete with the champion Shih Tzu who have been entered for the Best of Breed and Best of Opposite Sex to the Best of Breed awards. If there were more bitches entered than dogs and the Winners Dog goes Best of Winners, he earns the points won by the Winners Bitch instead of those he had previously won. If the Winners Dog or Bitch goes Best of Breed over several champions, these dogs (regardless of their sex) are added to the number of those he or she had already defeated in determining how many championship points the winner will earn that day. If the Winners Dog goes Best

At a prestigious show such as the Westminster Kennel Club, even the pros are a little tense while awaiting the judge's decision. Just don't convey your nervousness to your dog. (Backstage for Tammarie Larson)

of Opposite Sex over other champions, he can only add the male champions he defeats in determining his points that day; in a similar situation, the Winners Bitch can add only the bitch champions.

Only the Best of Breed Shih Tzu goes on to compete in the Toy Group with the Best of Breed winners from the other Toy breeds. If the Best of Breed Shih Tzu wins the Toy Group, it receives the largest number of points awarded to any breed in the Toy Group that day. Ribbons are given to the first through fourth place winners in the Toy Group, but only the dog placing first in the Toy Group advances to compete with the winners of each of the six other Groups for Best in Show.

If you are attending a dog show to observe Shih Tzu judging, plan to arrive early or check with someone who has entered a Shih Tzu to find out what time the breed will be judged. While you can still watch the Shih Tzu breed winner in the Group at the end of the day, many exhibitors leave once the breed has been judged and you will be unable to see all of the Shih Tzu if you arrive after breed judging. Before judging, the dogs can be found in the grooming area or in the parking area (many exhibitors have motor homes and groom their dogs there).

The show catalog, usually sold near the entrance to the show, will tell you where and when Shih Tzu are being judged and give you the names of the dogs entered and the names and addresses of their owners. You may also find Shih Tzu entered in obedience and agility competitions, if offered at that particular show. If you want to talk to the Shih Tzu exhibitors, remember that they are usually very busy getting their dogs ready for the ring before judging but will be happy to arrange to speak to you once the judging is over. Do not pet a Shih Tzu at a show without asking permission first; you may unknowingly undo hours of ring preparation or upset the dog just before judging. For the same reason, supervise your children carefully.

Familiarize yourself thoroughly with the breed standard and look at your dog objectively. The fact that he may have faults that would make him unsuitable for the show ring does not make him any less wonderful a companion. It simply means that you would be wasting your time and money trying to show him. If he is not suitable for the conformation ring and you would still like to

Begin teaching your Shih Tzu show puppy to stack and have his legs and mouth handled at a very young age. (Phyllis Schwab)

SHOULD YOU SHOW YOUR SHIH TZU?

First, be sure that your Shih Tzu is a good enough representative of the breed to be worthy of the show ring. Earning a championship is extremely difficult. In 1996, for example, the AKC granted individual registrations to more than 38,000 Shih Tzu. During that same year, only 211 Shih Tzu earned their championships! Another 14 earned their coveted ROM titles for producing the requisite number of champions that year, 14 earned obedience titles, and 6 earned agility titles. This is partly because most pet owners have no interest in showing their dogs, of course, but it also says something about just how difficult earning a title is.

take him to dog shows, you may want to try obedience or agility trials, which require considerable training and effort. They can be very rewarding activities for both you and your dog.

If you and your breeder believe that your dog is a quality Shih Tzu, ask other breeders to evaluate him. Sometimes, unfortunately, there may be "bad blood" between individual breeders. To ensure that you receive an honest evaluation, ask several breeders of show dogs to go over your dog. If only one of them thinks your Shih Tzu is not show quality, perhaps he is. If, on the other hand, everyone who examines him agrees that he has a particular fault or faults that would keep him from winning, he probably does.

You may also want to pay a professional handler for an evaluation of your dog.

No dog is without faults, so what is important is your dog's overall quality and attitude. Don't take the comments of the evaluators personally, even if the dog is one you have bred yourself. After all, you can't know what you need to improve in your breeding program unless you know what is wrong! The more open you are to honest criticism, the more you will learn and the more successful you will be.

SHOULD YOU HIRE A HANDLER?

If you have a quality Shih Tzu and would like to have him earn his AKC championship, you may or may not want to show him yourself. While there is nothing more rewarding than showing and finishing your own dog, particularly one you have bred, remember that it has taken the top professionals and breeder-handlers many years and untold hours to learn how to groom and present their dogs skillfully. They also, through experience, know what type of dog appeals to a particular judge. To compete with them, you must not only have a very good dog but also learn what they know. You *can* do it! Remember, every one of those confident, poised exhibitors you see collecting ribbons was once a novice just like you.

On the other hand, you may not have the time or the temperament to show your own dog. It may, in fact, be less costly to hire a handler because he or she will usually finish your dog faster than you can and save you the expense of going to the shows yourself. Some pampered pet Shih Tzu refuse to show well for their owners. They would rather play and act cute in the ring; or they think of all sorts of embarrassing ways to tell you they'd rather be home sleeping on the couch! In this case, or in the case of the owner who becomes an emotional basket case in the ring despite lots of practice, a more experienced handler may be a necessity.

Make lead-training a game, so your puppy will be an enthusiastic showman. Use bait or a squeaky toy, or play follow-the-leader with a lead-trained dog, to encourage the reluctant puppy to gait.

Spectators at their first dog show are often amazed that the dogs are so willing to lie quietly on the table after being groomed.

If you want to have someone else show your dog, investigate that person thoroughly. Don't just pick the handler that is doing the most winning or the one that has the lowest rates. Watch the handler at shows. Does he or she clearly love his or her client's dogs and treat them well? Do the dogs love the handler? What are the handler's kennel facilities like? Ask for references, and check them out.

Be sure that any arrangements you make with the handler are in writing and cover everything important to you. Your handler should be obligated to care for your dog properly and return it in at least as good a condition as he received it.

Remember that dog shows are your handler's livelihood, and that you are not his only client. You have a responsibility to pay your bills promptly, be clear about what you want, and understand that your dog cannot win at every show (particularly if he is immature or needs training or coat conditioning before he is really competitive). Do not take up hours of your handler's time discussing your Shih Tzu—this is time the handler could be spending grooming or training your dog!

If you feel uneasy about anything, however, do check it out before any permanent damage is done. Remember, you are entrusting a vulnerable and beloved animal into the care of a stranger and must do everything you can to ensure that you have made the right choice.

That said, there are many truly wonderful professionals who can do much more for your dog in the ring than you can, particularly if you decide to continue your dog's show career after he has completed his championship.

TRAINING YOUR PUPPY FOR THE RING

Whether or not you use a handler, you will likely be responsible for your show dog's early training. The most important thing is to establish a loving relationship with your dog from the very beginning, so that it will be happy in your presence and want to please you. The name of the game is, after all, dog *show,* and the judge is much more likely than not to award the ribbon to the enthusiastic showman that asks for it the most.

Some puppies, of course, are much more willing to stack than others! Just persevere, but remember to keep it fun.

confidently and quickly. In the ring, you will have very little time to set up your dog. Remember that the Shih Tzu is a relatively heavy small dog; it is very uncomfortable for him if you pick him up by his lead and his tail to put him on the table.

When setting or resetting your dog, reposition its feet by adjusting from the upper leg. Be sure that its feet point straight ahead, its elbows are tight to its body, and its rear is well angulated. Watch handlers stacking their dogs in the ring to see how the pros do it. You will spot a lot of tricks of the trade, like stretching the hind legs back rather far to improve the looks of a dog that is straight in the rear or long in back (this takes attention away from a back that is too long).

You can begin lead-training and exposure to a wide variety of people and situations with a very young puppy. Don't force it—use lots of praise and only mild corrections in training it to walk happily at your side on the lead and stand on the table. Have your friends go over your puppy as a judge would, and practice walking on both grass and hard surfaces, indoors and out. Shows are held in many different locations. Practice, don't drill. Make sure your puppy has fun during training sessions. Being too serious all the time can burn out a puppy (or an adult).

Ask exhibitors in your area to recommend a handling class where both you and your puppy can learn the ropes and where your puppy can become used to being around other dogs of all shapes and sizes. Read as many books about handling as you can to learn the "tricks of the trade," such as entering the ring first with a dog that loves to move or going to the end of the line with one that is slower or a bit insecure. Be sure to gait (move) your dog in a straight line; stop him and start again if he gets out of control. Practice stacking (posing) your dog in front of a mirror on the ground and on the table so that you can see what the judge is seeing. Do this over and over again until you can do it

Your show puppy will also have to be taught early to lie on his side on a table for grooming. Speak soothingly to calm him.

Learn how to show the bite if asked (open the lips, not the mouth—the judge wants to see how your dog's teeth meet and if all of them are there). Have friends practice examining the bite so that the dog will become accustomed to standing calmly while this is done.

Have a knowledgeable exhibitor watch you gait your dog at different speeds to determine what one shows off his gait to best advantage, and practice until this speed feels natural to you. Step out smoothly, beginning on the foot next to the dog, and do not take small, mincing steps. Remember that the breed standard specifies that the Shih Tzu is not to be shown "strung up," so practice gaiting until your Shih Tzu learns to walk at the correct pace on a loose lead with his head well up and his tail wagging. A dog with proper structure who is well trained should hold its head up naturally, with the lead used only for control.

If you want to bait your dog, select a food your dog loves and use it only when training for the ring. You will find that at first you will need to give small and frequent rewards, but later the dog will be willing to wait longer for gratification. Try baiting and posing in front of the mirror too, so that you can see just how to hold the lead and where to put the bait (generally down) to make your Shih Tzu look its most attractive. Be sure, when posing or baiting your dog, that you do not put your body between the dog and the judge—you are not the one he wants to see!

Above all, make showing fun for your dog. Do not keep him stacked for endless periods of time; let him play a bit when the judge is not watching so he will retain his enthusiasm. If it is a hot day, put him on a towel-wrapped ice pack or in the shade when he is not being examined so that he will not become overheated.

Once you feel confident about the basics—stacking your dog to best advantage on the ground and table, gaiting in various patterns at the speed that is best for your individual dog, and getting your dog to stop in front of

In gaiting, have an experienced exhibitor watch until you determine the speed that shows your particular dog to best advantage. Your own movement can enhance or detract from your dog. When the handler is taking tiny, mincing steps, so is the dog!

the judge in proper pose with his tail wagging—it is time to enter a few matches. These are a great training ground for both you and your dog and allow you both to overcome your nervousness and feeling of being "all thumbs."

AT THE SHOW

Once you are feeling confident, you're ready for the big time. AKC point shows must be entered about three weeks before the show, so get your name onto the mailing lists of the various show superintendents (listed in the *AKC Gazette Events Calendar*) in plenty of time so that you will be sure to receive the premium lists for shows in your area. Once you have entered you will receive, about a week before the show, a judging schedule telling you the time and ring for Shih Tzu judging. Bathe your dog the day before the show and gather all the equipment you will need to be sure you don't forget anything (including blue "freezer packs" to keep your Shih Tzu cool on a hot

day). Do not feed your dog the morning of the show, so that he will be alert and responsive to the bait. Allow plenty of time to get to the show (including time to get lost) and groom your dog for the ring. Locate your ring when you arrive and pick up your armband from the ring steward at ringside before judging. Remember that you are responsible for getting to the ring on time.

Give your dog an opportunity to eliminate before he enters the ring. Watch the judge's ring procedures before your class is called so that you will know what is expected of you (e.g., which gaiting pattern is used?; are there any obstacles that might trip you?; will you have to open your own dog's mouth?; etc.).

When it is your turn to enter the ring, be sure your Shih Tzu is well groomed and that you yourself look professional. Wear shoes with nonskid soles (white ones can distract a judge's attention from a less than perfect gait) and attractive clothing that will not interfere with showing your dog—a suit and

When the handler is moving too rapidly the dog is lagging and holding its head improperly. The same dog presents a very different picture when moved at the proper speed, (which is a trot, not a gallop), exhibiting correct head carriage and good reach and drive. (Richard Paquette)

Set your dog up in front of a mirror so that you can see exactly what the judge sees. These four pictures show the same dog from the judge's angle. The dog at the upper left is stacked correctly. When it leans forward into the lead even slightly (upper right), the outline is not as appealing. When it leans well forward and drops its head (lower right), the dog looks terrible! At the lower left, it is lifting one front foot (on the judge's side, naturally), throwing off the whole picture.

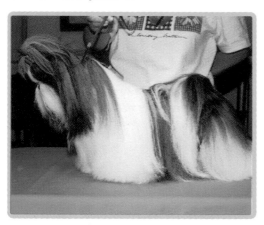

tie for men and culottes or other comfortable but attractive clothes for women. Don't wear dangling jewelry, long skirts that flap in front of the dog's eyes, or short shorts, and be sure you have plenty of pockets to hold brush, comb, and bait.

Look confident, as if you know that you have the best dog there. Pay careful attention to the judge's instructions once you have entered the ring, and be sure to watch both the judge and your dog at all times. By now you should have learned how to present your dog smoothly and to its best advantage, showing off its strong points and (unobtrusively) covering up its faults.

The judge has only about two minutes per dog, so you want your Shih Tzu to be looking its very best whenever he glances at it, not just during the individual examination. Also, remember that there may well be other judges or exhibitors watching.

First and last impressions are especially critical. You may want to use bait or a small squeaky toy to catch your dog's attention and make him look animated. Spend some time stroking him and talking to him so that he is calm, happy, and assured.

Win or lose, be a good sport. Don't run up on the person in front of you in the ring or drop bait on the ground to distract the next dog, be sure to congratulate the winners and *always* praise your dog.

When you stack your Shih Tzu, on the ground or on the table, put the lead around your neck so that you will have both hands free to work with the dog. Drop the dog from under the chin, then check to see that the front feet are pointing straight ahead and feel to see that the front and rear legs are properly positioned. Put the tail correctly over the back and brush the dog out if necessary, stroking and talking to it soothingly so that the dog will be relaxed. Once the dog is stacked correctly, you can take the lead in your right hand and remove your left, being watchful and ready to make smooth but instantaneous adjustments if your dog shifts position.

Practice gaiting your dog on many different surfaces and in different patterns, keeping the dog between you and the judge. Talk to him to keep him happy and alert.

Train your dog to come to a stop in front of the judge with head well up, topline level, and all four feet in proper position.

Grooming skills are an important part of showing in conformation. If you are a novice, you must be willing and able to follow your breeder's instructions or hire a professional handler to deal with coat care. (Earl Takahashi)

GROOMING THE SHOW SHIH TZU

Just as with a pet Shih Tzu, accustom your show puppy to grooming at an early age and to accept bathing readily. Make the grooming sessions fun. Never stop because the dog is misbehaving—you want to stop a grooming session while the dog is behaving, rather than have it control when you stop. If you find yourself getting really upset, call a halt to the session and resume later. Talk soothingly to your dog as you work and praise it for behaving. This works much better than making grooming a contest of the wills.

It is critical that you keep your show puppy's nails cut short and the hair trimmed ing it out. You want to remove only dead, never live, hair. If you are removing a lot of hair on the brush, you are not dematting correctly. Do not let your show dog play with other dogs or run on synthetic carpeting or in underbrush. Many people keep their dogs in exercise pens with floor grates during their show careers to prevent coat damage.

Always use scissors to cut out the latex bands in the topknot so that you do not remove hair. If your dog tends to rub its face, products such as Wella Kolestral (human), Shaw's Royal Coatalin (canine), or a drop of Zoto's Bain de Terre Recovery Complex (available at a beauty supply store) can be worked

Never brush your dog dry, as you will break hair. Always spray first lightly with a mixture of cream rinse and water.

level with its footpads. Overly long nails cause the feet to splay and keep the dog from moving properly.

One of the most important things to learn if you are planning to show your dog is the proper brushing technique. Your Shih Tzu should be brushed every day and bathed weekly to ensure that mats do not form. When you brush, brush carefully in layers from the bottom up, being sure that you brush all the way down to the skin. Whenever you hit a mat (you will feel the resistance to the brush), however small, break it apart carefully with your fingers before brush-

into the facial hair to provide extra protection against breakage. Some exhibitors braid the topknot or band it in two sections on either side of the head rather than in the center to avoid having the bands in the same place between shows as they are during exhibition. Others braid the mustache or wrap and band it to keep it dry, leaving the hairs at the inside corner of the eye free to wick away moisture. Having your dog drink from a water bottle helps to keep the face dry. Position the bottle high enough so that the dog will have to stretch its neck to reach for it.

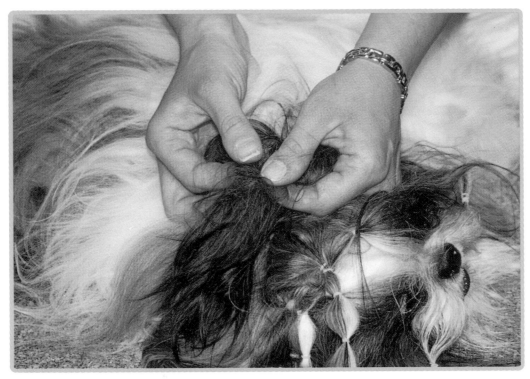

When you hit a mat, break it apart with your fingers before attempting to brush it out. Attack large mats from the outer edges.

Train your dog to lie on its side for grooming. The hair on the legs should be brushed toward the body.

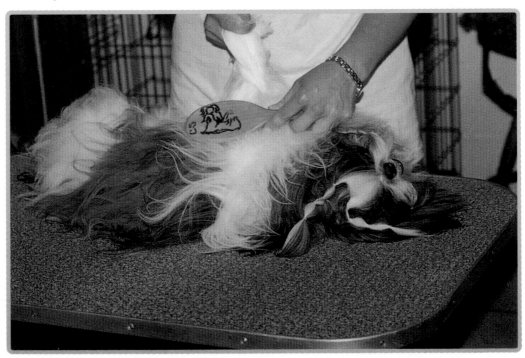

Brush the dog in layers, getting all the way down to the skin, and do not flip the brush up when you reach the end of the coat.

If you regularly remove excess hair from the ear canal, applying a little ear powder first will make the job easier.

This is just one of the many ways of banding the head of a show Shih Tzu to preserve the hair and keep it dry.

Remove only the hair inside the ear canal. There are no nerves there, so if your Shih Tzu fusses it is only because it tickles.

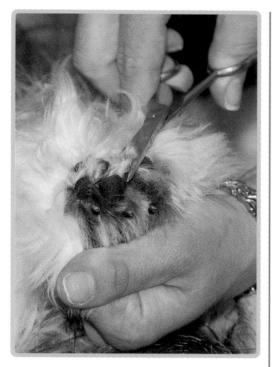

Keep your Shih Tzu's nails cut short so his feet will not splay and trim any excess hair from between the pads of the feet.

Cleaning out the hair between the footpads gives your dog good footing and keeps painful mats from forming there.

Trim only a clean dog. Before trimming, brush the coat out and use a knitting needle to part the hair along the back. Follow the spine, then comb. You can adjust the part slightly to compensate for a less-than-level topline.

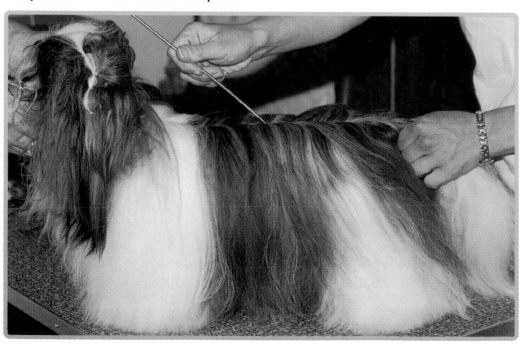

Trim the hair on all four legs in layers, clipping back excess hair to avoid cutting the wrong thing. Comb before cutting.

Trim the hair level with the table. Adjust the cut wider on the outside and narrower on the inside to widen a narrow front or rear.

Comb the outer hair down and trim again for a neat, finished appearance. Once all four legs have been trimmed, trim the side coat level with the table. Be sure to stack the dog in proper show pose so your trim will look correct in the ring.

The anal area should also be trimmed for neatness. This also shortens the back of the dog and improves the look of the tailset.

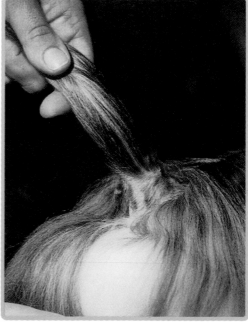

As you can see from these before (above) and after (below) photos, ironing the coat with a special padded iron made for dogs removes any waves from the hair. This straightening adds length to the coat and gives it a finished appearance. Ironing also gives the coat more shine.

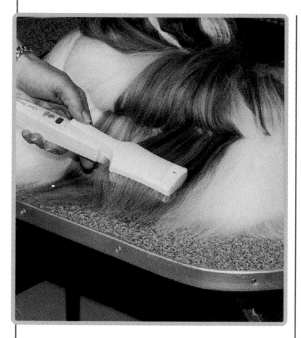

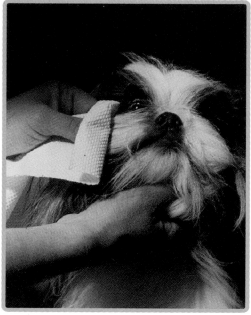

With a special padded iron made for dogs, iron a small section at a time, dampening the hair first. Leaving the iron on the coat too long can burn the hair, so be careful.

Doing up the face is perhaps the most challenging part of preparing your Shih Tzu for the show ring. First, clean the mustache with a self-rinse shampoo and dry it thoroughly.

Band a tiny strip of hair just under the inner corner of each eye in absorbent paper. This will help keep the face dry until showtime.

Remove the hairbands with surgical scissors. This will keep you from removing unnecessary hair along with the bands.

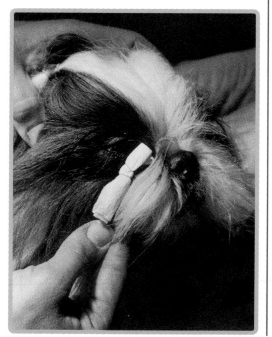

Have your breeder or someone else expert in show grooming demonstrate the proper brushing technique. When you get to the ends of the coat, do not scoop the bottom of the brush upward. Rather, rotate the brush away from the coat from the top, so that you do not catch and break off the ends of the coat. Because a damp coat is more resilient and less likely to break, *never* brush the coat without lightly spraying it with a mixture of conditioner and water. Most exhibitors find it better to use a conditioner to protect the coat than to put the dog down in oil, as the oil collects dirt and is difficult to wash out

Whiten and dry the blaze and mustache with cornstarch (applied with a soft brush), being sure to brush it out thoroughly.

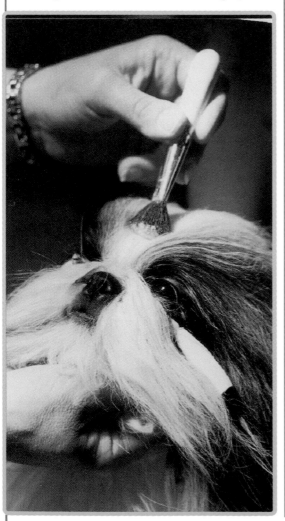

completely. Oil treatments seem to create more problems than they solve in a soft-textured coat. Leave more conditioner in the coat between shows than when you are bathing the dog out for a show. If you find that the dog's coat is becoming limp from overconditioning, you may want to use a super cleansing shampoo or change shampoos and rinses for a time.

When you bathe the dog, do not scrub. Work the shampoo gently through the coat with your fingers, and shampoo twice, rinsing thoroughly each time. If your dog's coat is extremely soft (it's best to avoid this texture unless you are experienced), you may want to add some texturizing shampoo to your regular shampoo to make it easier to manage. You may want to use a tearless whitening shampoo on the facial hair and feet. Use a good conditioner after washing your dog before a show. You will have to experiment to determine just how much conditioner to leave in the coat to give it the best appearance.

There is no one magic shampoo or cream rinse for every Shih Tzu—different textured coats require different products. Ask your breeder or other exhibitors showing dogs with coat textures similar to yours for tips on specific products to use.

Be especially careful to control any flea problems immediately. Just one flea bite can undo months of conditioning in a dog with sensitive skin.

When you are blow drying your dog, be sure the dryer is not set on a high temperature that will cause damage to the coat or burn the dog's skin. Dry the dog in layers from the bottom up, just as you brush. If the dog has a very thick, bushy coat, you can tame it down by blowing in the direction of the hair growth. If you want to add thickness, brush in the opposite direction from the way the hair grows.

Once your dog is bathed and dry, with its nails and footpads trimmed, you are ready for final show preparation. You can trim the feet, anal area, and sidecoat after the bath, but you will probably have to do a bit of touch-up trimming at the show.

The basic topknot is a good one for a dog with a correct head, but there are various tricks used by skilled groomers to camouflage a head that is less than perfect. Adding extra bands to the topknot gives additional height to a flat skull, and added back banding gives the appearance of a longer neck. An extreme pouf in the front of the topknot shortens a longer nose. A wider topknot seems to widen a narrow head, while a narrower topknot makes a very broad head look narrower. Teasing the mustache gives the appearance of more cushioning on the muzzle. A puppy topknot is generally set further forward on the skull to catch all of the short hair in the band. You will have to experiment with various topknot styles to see which is best for your own dog. When trimming the feet, you can make adjustments to make the chest or the rear look wider or narrower. Again, just how you trim depends upon the particular dog, remembering that the breed standard calls for the judge to penalize excessive trimming. You need to know both the standard and your dog very well to do the best job.

Part the hair above the nose and rub on a little gel with your finger to make the hair easier to handle and control stray wisps.

Use your knitting needle or the handle on your comb to part the hair to form the front half of the circle that will make the topknot.

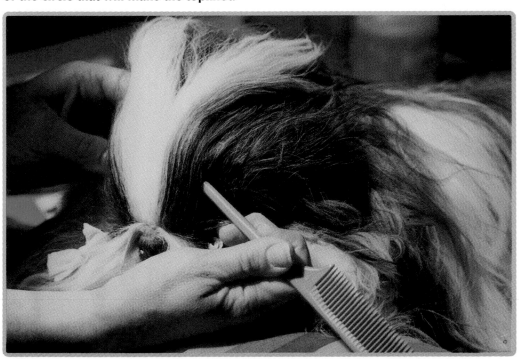

KEEPING THE FACE WHITE

Keeping the facial hair of some Shih Tzu white is a serious problem. There is some indication that a tendency to stain may be genetic. Sometimes, such a stain is caused by the food or water, by the fact that some dog's faces seem to be perpetually wet, or by an eye infection. Be sure to use food and treats that have no added color. If your tap water has a high iron content, it will cause the face to stain, so use bottled distilled water. You may want to add a capful of raw apple cider vinegar (available in a health food store) to one quart of distilled water for your dog to drink; some people contend that it not only helps keep the face white but also repels fleas by making the dog's skin slightly acidic. Some people supplement with zinc or 100–200 mg. per day of vitamin C to help control face stain. To help open blocked tear ducts (which contribute to face stain), massage the bridge of the puppy's nose under his eyes with your thumb and forefinger once or twice a day, gradually tapering off to once or twice a week. If the facial staining is caused by an eye inflammation, it may be improved by using Tetracycline ointment in your dog's eyes, as your vet recommends. Finally, clean the facial area with a cotton ball moistened with a solution of one part distilled water to one part 3% hydrogen peroxide. Be sure not to get this into the dog's eyes. Using corn starch applied with a baby toothbrush on the dog's mustache may also help to keep the face dry and white, but not if your dog is one of those who tears when you use powder near his eyes, so use your own judgment.

With the comb, lightly tease the back of this section. The more you tease, the more pouf the topknot will have. Smooth out the front of the topknot before banding it.

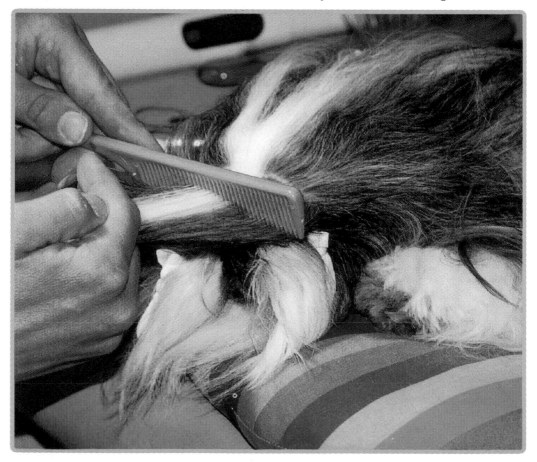

Band the front half of the topknot. Using a chin pillow while making the topknot will give you better control over your dog.

Take two small sections of hair from the back of this section and pull. This poufs the topknot and holds it tight to the skull.

Use your knitting needle to make the back half of the circle. How wide the topknot is depends on the dog's head, but do not put any of the hair on the ears into the topknot.

Band the back section, and take two tiny pieces of hair from the front of this section and pull, as you did when doing the front.

Fasten the two sections together, hiding the bands with a bow. The size and color of the bow should enhance your particular dog.

Add one or more bands to each section. The more bands, the longer the neck will appear.

Use a curling iron on the topknot to keep it from falling over the eyes. Again, the higher the pouf, the longer the neck will seem.

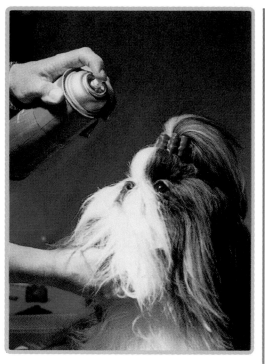

Once the curls have set, backcomb lightly, comb smooth, and spray to set. Be sure not to get hairspray into your dog's eyes.

With the lead on, do a final brushing, smoothing the hair around the lead. Spray lightly to control static electricity.

Just before ringtime, part the hair around the neck before putting on the lead, which should rest just above the Adam's apple.

Remove the paper at the eye corners at the very last minute, brush again, and your dog is ready for the ring. Isn't she pretty?

Judging the Shih Tzu

Most conformation judges are former breeders, exhibitors, or professional handlers with many years of experience in dogs. However, not all judges or prospective judges have intimate, hands-on knowledge of our particular breed. When judging the Shih Tzu, you must memorize the breed standard and then learn to apply this standard to real dogs. The ASTC hopes that the *Illustrated Guide to the Shih Tzu Standard* will help you to better understand the breed standard (the description of the always elusive perfect Shih Tzu) and apply it in your judging. Check the *AKC Gazette Events Calendar* to see when judges' seminars on our breed will be held in your area, attend as many dog shows as you can, and contact the ASTC for the name of the breeder-judge mentor in your area to arrange for a hands-on individualized learning experience. In addition, you may want to purchase copies of the video tape of the 1995 ASTC Breeder Education Symposium on the Shih Tzu standard, which is available to judges and prospective judges.

Because the Shih Tzu head is so extreme, it has a tendency to revert rather quickly to generic canine type. Heads narrow and flatten, eyes become smaller, muzzles lengthen, stops disappear, and bites become narrow and scissor, or even overshot. Because the Shih Tzu head and expression are such a great part of its unique appeal, it is very important for breeders, exhibitors and judges to pay particular attention to head type as well as overall soundness and style. The Shih Tzu, like many other breeds, has and undoubtedly will continue to go through fads, ranging from the huge-headed, barrel-chested, low-stationed Shih Tzu, so common in the breed's early years, to the slab-sided, pea-headed giraffes that were the extreme result of breeders' attempts to make the breed "more stylish." Even if most of the dogs in your ring on a particular day reflect the fad-of-the-minute, be disciplined and principled enough to judge according to the breed standard, which calls for an overall well-balanced dog. Remember that your decisions will have a great impact on the dogs that will be extensively used for breeding in the future, and that exaggerated fads can destroy breed type—the essence of the breed as described in the standard. You should not be rewarding breeders who are not breeding to the standard.

When you are judging Shih Tzu on a very hot day, remember that this is a short-faced, heavily coated bread that does not take the heat well. Even if you must alter your customary ring procedure, we ask that you try to remember to set the class up in the shade and place the table on which you will examine the dogs in the shade as well, for the welfare of the dogs. Black and black and white Shih Tzu seem especially susceptible to heat stroke when made to stand in the sun for long periods of time because dark coats absorb more heat than lighter-colored ones.

EXAMINING THE SHIH TZU ON THE TABLE

Examining a Toy dog such as the Shih Tzu at eye-level on a table gives you the opportunity to determine its true proportion and balance, which can be concealed by grass and by perspective. Are the dog's individual features in correct proportion to one another, creating an overall pleasing appearance? You may wish to drop the front to see if the elbows

A warm, sweet expression—created by the proper combination of head shape, muzzle and eye placement, muzzle cushioning, and eye shape and color—is a distinguishing characteristic of our breed. (Earl Takahashi)

are properly tight to the chest. Does the dog have sufficient depth and breadth of chest for its size? You should be able to insert your hand between its front legs. Are the shoulders well-laid back, and do they fit smoothly into the body? Is the rear angulation in balance with the forequarters? Are topline, coat texture, and tailset correct, and is the dog in good physical condition?

Is the head broad and round and the muzzle square, well-cushioned, and set no lower than the bottom eye rim? Is there a definite stop? Are the eyes large, round, dark, and set well apart, without showing excessive eye white? (White-ringed eyes or excessive eye white in the inside corners of the eyes detract from the desired warm, soft expression.) One disturbing trend noted by many breeder-judges is the tendency toward a smaller, almond-shaped eye, so be sure that the eyes are round, full, and dark. It is more important that the jaw be broad and wide and that the chin not recede than that

of a broader head, shorter nose, and deeper stop than actually exists. Multiple bands (hidden under a bow and curled, teased hair) can create the illusion of more neck or dome, and teasing of the mustache gives the appearance of muzzle cushioning. You must use your hands (hopefully without totally destroying the topknot) to feel what is under the hair and determine whether or not the dog you are examining would have the same sweet, wide-eyed expression if it had not been groomed so skillfully.

These photos are of the same Shih Tzu on the same day, but the continuation of the white shawl from back to table on one side gives the optical illusion of a more elegant outline in the top photo. Be aware of the false impressions that can be created by markings.

MOVEMENT

It is relatively easy for a skilled handler to stack a Shih Tzu so that it appears to be an excellent specimen. You must therefore be sure to look at the dogs carefully on the ground as well as on the table. How do they stand when they are relaxed and on a loose lead? If the handler is stringing a dog up, he or she may be trying to camouflage poor front assembly. Also, when a dog is strung up, it cannot move freely as it should.

all of the teeth be present and in perfect alignment. Remember that without the unique Oriental expression so characteristic of our breed throughout its history, the Shih Tzu is just another dog.

It is easy for a skilled groomer to create the impression of a correct head through grooming techniques. A very poufed, poodle-like topknot can give the impression

When gaiting a class of Shih Tzu, both individually and as a group, remember that our standard calls for the dog to be moved at its own natural speed, neither raced nor strung up. (The standard does not call for a dead loose lead, and slight tension on the lead to control the dog is not considered strung up.) This will enable you to determine whether the dog's structure allows it to move smoothly and effortlessly with its head held up naturally.

While the well-moving Shih Tzu, especially a young puppy with a coat that has not yet reached the floor, may appear to have a very slight roll (due to the movement of its coat and its broad chest, not to being out at the elbows or to bowed front legs), it should never bounce or bob. Jerky movement generally indicates that the front and rear are not in balance, or that the shoulder assembly is incorrect.

The topline should be level while standing and moving. The dog should not be high in the rear; neither should its topline slope downward from withers to tail like a Sporting dog. The Shih Tzu should carry its tail well over the back in a teacup handle, neither flagging like a beagle nor laying its tail flat over its back like a Pekingese. A tail that is set too low will make the topline appear roached and the back seem longer.

The front legs should be extended well out (but not high up in an inefficient, prancing manner) straight in front of the dog from under the heaviest part of the body when moving, not from in front of the chest as is the case with a shoulder assembly placed too far forward. The front legs should not swing outward before hitting the ground, as do those of a Pekingese. The latter movement is very inefficient. When the front and rear are not in balance, a Shih Tzu may sidewind. If the rear is more angulated than the front, it may kick its rear legs up high in a very showy fashion, without covering much ground. This is incorrect. A too-long neck or a too-short back also interfere with proper front reach and rear drive. Although the legs converge as speed increases, the Shih Tzu should never singletrack. Both rear pads should be seen with some lateral spacing between them.

The Shih Tzu's front and rear must be in proper balance for correct movement. When viewed from the side, the Shih Tzu exhibits good reach and drive and the correct level topline. Speed is not the same as reach and drive; proper Shih Tzu movement is a trot, not a gallop. If the handler of a dog lacking front reach pulls the head back over the shoulders on a tight lead and races the dog, its front reach may appear better than it actually is. The head carriage, however, will be incorrect. (Janine for Isabelle Beaulne)

Nose, muzzle, lip, and eyerim pigment (except on blue or liver dogs) should be very dark. (James Hall)

COLOR, COAT, AND PRESENTATION

All colors are permissible in our breed and should be considered *equally*. Take the additional time needed to carefully examine the head and expression on a black or black-masked dog, and do not be put off by the lighter eyes and pigment of liver or blue Shih Tzu. Markings can create deceptive optical illusions; be aware of them. A wide blaze will make the head appear broader, and a wide white shawl will shorten the back. Black "eye stripes" on either side of a wide blaze tend to dramatize the typical Shih Tzu expression, making the eyes look wider, fuller, and more expressive. Knowing this, many breeders keep dogs with these markings for the show ring over dogs of equal quality without the "flash." The fact that such markings are more common in your ring does not mean that they are more desirable in terms of the standard. Do not let color and markings influence your decision about the merits of a particular dog.

Coat texture is as important as coat color is not. The Shih Tzu is a double-coated breed. Although a slight wave is permissible, the coat should not be curly, and a sparse or single coat is considered a fault. Most breeders prefer a sturdy coat texture, particularly in terms of breeding—extremely soft, cottony coats are dreadful for even an experienced exhibitor to maintain and impossible for a pet owner to deal with. So much can be done these days with texturizing shampoos and rinses, ironing, etc., that it is difficult to tell exactly which dog naturally possesses proper texture. Except in a sparsely coated dog unable to grow luxurious hair, the amount of coat is often due to grooming expertise.

A spectacular coat and skilled trimming can hide a multitude of structural faults, however. Although excessive trimming is faulted in the breed standard, occasionally an unethical groomer will thin or shave the hair under the shawl to give the appearance

Take time to examine the heads of solid-colored dogs thoroughly, such as this black-masked gold Shih Tzu. It is harder to determine whether or not solid-colored Shih Tzu have the proper head and expression, but they should not be ignored. (June Selby)

These two Shih Tzu have similar heads, but the dog on the right has more white, making it appear to have a broader head and muzzle. Do not be deceived by such optical illusions and remember that all markings are equally acceptable. (Isabelle Beaulne)

of more neck. Also, chest hair is sometimes thinned to give the appearance of shorter overall length. It is critical to examine what lies under all the hair.

Coat and grooming alone should not a winner make, although it may be the deciding factor between two equally sound and typey Shih Tzu. Although the name of the game is dog "show," and skillful grooming has become common, try not to penalize the novice exhibitor with a quality animal as long as the coat is clean, well-brushed, and of acceptable quantity and texture.

GENERAL COMMENTS

Of course, you should be especially courteous to novice exhibitors, so that they will find the world of dog shows a pleasant experience. Do the same for novice dogs, as a heavy-handed examination or dangling jewelry can ruin a potential winner forever. Every exhibitor has paid the same entry fee and should not be shortchanged, even if his dog is not in serious contention. You will, of course, have your individual interpretation of our breed standard, but you will inevitably be criticized unless you judge the dogs, not

These five photos, taken before the making of topknots became an art, clearly show various types of Shih Tzu heads. Clockwise, the first dog, unlike the other four Shih Tzu pictured, has the correct broad, round head and soft expression. The second dog has a "Peke" type head with an extremely short muzzle and lack of topskull. The third dog has a too narrow head, muzzle, and jaw, and close-set eyes. In the fourth dog, the lower jaw is weak, detracting from the desired expression. The fifth dog's head has too much dome and he shows excessive eye white. It is hard to determine head and expression in the ring today due to skillful grooming, so be sure to check what is under the topknot. (Top right: Larry Kalstone for Jo Ann White)

The topknot can be banded in such a way as to give the appearance of additional dome and to increase neck length. (Peter J. Rogers III)

the owners. Judge each dog as it appears on a particular day, not on the basis of its past record. A puppy should be considered equally with an adult, as you are judging on the day, not on the basis of how the youngster will look a year or so from now! Do not fault-judge, or you will miss the forest for the trees.

A truly quality Shih Tzu should catch your eye the minute it enters the ring (allowing, of course, for serious faults that may be camouflaged by grooming or handling skills prior to a detailed examination). It should be typey, sound, stylish, and in good physical condition and exhibit a friendly, outgoing, and happy temperament. Do nothing in your judging that would detract from the importance of these qualities, for they are what make our breed both a joy to watch in the show ring and a delightful companion.

A young Shih Tzu whose side-coat just reaches the elbows can appear to be out at the elbows simply because of its coat. Again, examine under the hair for structure. (Phyllis Schwab)

Rewarding Activities for You and Your Shih Tzu

€ven if it is not appropriate for the conformation ring, your Shih Tzu doesn't have to be a couch potato! There are many enjoyable and satisfying activities for you and your pet in the wonderful world of dogs.

THE SHIH TZU IN OBEDIENCE

Any AKC-registered purebred Shih Tzu over six months of age, including spayed females and altered males, can participate in AKC obedience trials and earn obedience titles. Obedience training is rewarding for you and your dog, whether or not you ever become involved in competition, because it teaches your pet to be well behaved. Many obedience clubs offer training classes. If you want to give your dog basic obedience training without learning the finer points of competitive obedience, beginning obedience classes are often offered as part of the adult education program of your local school district. Because the Shih Tzu trains best under a system of praise, rather than harsh correction, it is important to visit a class you are considering before you enroll, to be sure that the methods used are suitable for a small dog. Many Shih Tzu owners have found using a "clicker" helpful in training.

AKC obedience competition is divided into three levels of increasing difficulty. To earn a title, the dog must successfully perform the exercises required at that level at three separate shows under three different judges, scoring at least 170 of a possible 200 points and receiving more than 50% of the possible points for each exercise. The first level, novice, requires a dog to heel both on and off leash at varying speeds (including an on-lead figure-eight around two ring stewards), to stay off-leash in both the sit and down position with a group of other dogs when told to do so, to stand for examination by the judge with the handler six feet away, and to come when called. The novice obedience title is Companion Dog (CD).

A dog successfully competing in the second level, or open, earns a Companion Dog Excellent (CDX) title by performing many of the same exercises for longer periods and without a leash, plus more difficult ones such as dropping in the middle of the recall, negotiating the broad jump, and retrieving on the flat and over a high jump. To earn a Utility Dog (UD) title, your Shih Tzu must perform even more difficult exercises, including a scent exercise in which he determines which of a group of articles his owner has handled and retrieves this article.

A Utility Dog that goes on to qualify for legs in both open and utility B classes at the same show in ten shows earns the title Utility Dog Excellent (UDX), and Utility Dogs that rank first or second in open B or utility B classes earn points toward the highly coveted Obedience Trial Champion (OTCh.) title. Only three Shih Tzu have won the OTCh. title, which requires 100 points: OTCh. Pat Tez Lu Yen Ce; OTCh. Pat Tez Yoshiko; and OTCh. Helen's Brandy. Brandy was also is the only Shih Tzu to have won an AKC tracking title (TD), by demonstrating his ability to recognize and follow human scent.

If you think you might want to purchase a Shih Tzu with the goal of showing in obedience, evaluate its temperament carefully. It should be bright, unafraid, and eager to please. Very nervous or extremely dominant dogs are generally much more difficult, if not impossible, to obedience train. Working in obedience is also often very beneficial to build confidence and the human-animal bond in rescue dogs.

There are many games you can play with your puppy that will help him in obedience work later on, especially teaching him to come when called only once. Do not keep repeating the command or he will learn to ignore it. Reward him when he comes and *never* chase him when he does not or he will think disobeying is a fun game. One good way to train your puppy to come is by getting down on his level, with a friend doing the same at the opposite end of the room. Clap your hands and call him to each of you in turn, rewarding him with treats, play, and praise, especially when he comes quickly. *Never* scold your puppy for coming to you, even when you didn't call him. Teach your puppy to retrieve a toy when you toss it and release it into your hand. Use another toy to entice him to return to you with the first one.

When training your Shih Tzu to heel, practice walking naturally with a shorter than normal stride with your feet pointing straight ahead. Step out on your right foot, being sure you have your dog's attention first. Footwork will help cue your dog. (Cindy Rhodes)

Many trainers, particularly at the advanced level, choose to use hand signals rather than voice commands. (Cindy Rhodes)

Footwork is extremely important in working with a small dog. In doing the figure eight, for example, be careful to keep your feet side by side going around the curves, so that your dog does not have to go wide or lag to avoid your swinging feet.

You can teach your puppy to walk on a leash on your left side, to stand for examination, to stay, and to jump an obstacle when you say "over." If your puppy seems nervous about standing for examination by a stranger, teach the exercise first with him sitting down. This will make him feel less insecure. When first training your dog on the bar jump or high jump, set it at the lowest possible level and let your dog smell and examine the jump before beginning your approach. Start at least eight feet away from the jump. To proceed beyond the novice level, have your dog's hips x-rayed to be sure that he is able to withstand the physical stress of jumping.

Many dogs have won both championships and obedience titles and recognize the difference between training for the two types of competition by the different leashes you use. In obedience, unlike in conformation, any dog performing successfully earns a leg toward an obedience title, although only the highest scoring dogs win ribbons. Obedience competition therefore tends to be much friend-lier and less competitive, except at the highest levels. In both rings, Shih Tzu revel in the praise they receive for a successful performance. They are real hams.

The biggest problem with training a Shih Tzu for obedience is its tendency to engage in cute but undesirable antics. A Shih Tzu that responds to the command "down" by flipping over on its back, kissing the air, and wagging its entire body, or one that inches under the shade of a table on its belly on a hot day, can be frustrating, to say the least. The judge and the other exhibitors may smile, but this won't earn your dog its title! Because Shih Tzu are so smart, they sometimes figure out that they can get away with such tricks in the show ring because you can't correct them. (Some owners arrange for mock shows in obedience class so their Shih Tzu never know when they will be subjected to a correction). Match shows are also good practice for the real thing. To learn just what is expected of you and your dog in obedience, write to the AKC at 5580 Centerview Drive, Raleigh, NC 27606 for a copy of *Obedience Regulations.*

Your dog should wear a well-fitting plain buckle or slip collar without tags. A small-link metal chain choke collar works well on a Shih Tzu because it is less likely to become

In the long sit and long down exercises, your Shih Tzu will have to remain in place with the other dogs in his class. At more advanced levels of competition, the dogs have to stay longer with the owners out of sight. This photo shows why it is important to accustom your Shih Tzu to interacting with dogs of different shapes and sizes! (Doris Pletl)

When recalling your dog from in front of the jump, remember that his depth perception is poor. If you stand too close to the jump, he may refuse to go over because he is afraid he will jump into you.

The scent discrimination exercise requires your dog to select the object handled by his owner from a group of similar objects and retrieve it. Begin by tying down the unscented articles to a rubber mat so that the scented article is the only one the dog will be able to remove. You might also initially rub the scented article with cheese or a piece of hot dog to encourage your dog to pick it up. Later, have other people handle the articles you have not touched so that your dog will discriminate between your scent and others, rather than your scent and no scent. (Cindy Rhodes)

tangled in the hair. While you can use as much praise and food as you like in training, in the obedience ring you can praise your dog only between exercises, and you cannot use bait in the ring or pick up your dog and carry it at any time. Bitches in season cannot compete, because they distract the other dogs. Disciplining your dog in the ring is cause for immediate disqualification.

In obedience (or any other dog activity), you should learn to read your dog's body language and never do anything to your dog that you do not feel is okay, no matter who tells you differently. Endless drilling is another no-no. It will bore your dog and it'll come to hate obedience. Consistency is also extremely important in obedience training.

When your dog comes to you (top), he should sit directly in front of you close to your feet until you command him (bottom left) to "finish." When finishing this or any other exercise (bottom right), be sure your dog sits close to your left side facing straight ahead. (Cindy Rhodes)

Begin training your dog to retrieve as a puppy, using toys. Be sure to get a dumbbell sized for a small dog, with end pieces large enough for him to get his lower jaw under the narrow center rod easily.

Because teaching your dog to pick up an object on command is one of the most difficult exercises in obedience, never punish him for putting something into his mouth by yelling at him or grabbing at him. Calmly substitute an appropriate object. (Cindy Rhodes)

Remember that a small dog going over the broad jump can see only the first board and doesn't know how far he should jump. Begin with only one board. When you add the second one, place the bar from the bar jump on two cans in the center of the boards so the dog will jump high enough to clear both boards and will not land between them. It is better to teach good habits than to break bad ones. (Cindy Rhodes)

When first training your dog on the bar or high jumps, set the jump as low as possible and take him over on a lead. Praise him when he commits to the jump ("Let's go") and while he is jumping ("Over"), not just when he is finished.

When training your dog to retrieve over the high jump, practice throwing the dumbbell in a low arc to the same spot every time (at least eight feet on the other side of the jump). This will help focus your dog's attention. (Cindy Rhodes)

THE SHIH TZU IN AGILITY

The competitive canine performance sport of agility is meant to be fun for you and your dog. It is perhaps the ultimate experience in the human-animal bond. It began in Great Britain in 1978 as an exhibition at the world-famous Crufts dog show and became an official AKC performance event in 1994. Today it is the fastest growing addition to the sport of dogs. A dog doesn't have to be large to win in agility. This is a sport for young and old, large and small—dogs and handlers.

Use animated praise, food, and toys to train your dog for agility. Never use the word "no" or heavy-handed corrections when training for agility ("uh-uh" or a grunt will do), as self-confidence is one of the most important qualities of the good agility dog. Practice frequently, but only do each exercise two or three times. Endless drilling can quench your dog's enthusiasm.

To compete in agility, your dog should be physically sound. Spayed bitches and neutered males can compete, but bitches in season cannot participate. The rules of the

Agility trials are the height of canine competition! The first few times your dog tries the A-frame, have a friend as a spotter on the other side of the apparatus so that your dog will not be tempted to jump off on the side away from you. (Phyllis Celmer)

various organizations offering agility competition vary slightly, although they are generally similar. The jump heights, based on the height of the dog at the withers, differ among different organizations. Among the organizations offering agility titles are the American Kennel Club, the National Association of Dog Agility Council, the United Kennel Club, and the U.S. Dog Agility Association. The latter is the most competitive and challenging. Dogs must be 12 months old to compete in AKC agility trials and 18 months old to compete in USDAA trials. In AKC

speed and any deductions for non-disqualifying faults. A perfect score is 100; a score of 85 with no disqualifying deductions is required to earn a leg. During the actual running of the course, there should be no contact between owner and dog, either hand or leash, and the owner cannot touch any of the obstacles.

While formal obedience training is not necessary for agility, it is helpful if your Shih Tzu is familiar with the commands "sit," "down," "stay," and "come." The agility course is complex. The dog's tasks including

When beginning agility training, offer your dog an instantaneous reward for going over a jump or through the tire (clicker training works here, too). This will make for a swift and enthusiastic performance later on. (Catherine A. Haake for Joan Condon)

agility trials, a dog must earn three qualifying scores (legs) under two different judges to earn an agility title. Titles begin at an elementary level and progress to more advanced levels. The AKC agility titles offered, in ascending order of difficulty are: Novice Agility (NA), Open Agility (OA), Agility Excellent (AX), and Master Agility Excellent (MX). Scoring is figured based upon

walking over a bridge (dog walk) and an A-frame; negotiating a teeter totter (seesaw); jumping through a circle, tire, or window and over broad and various other jumps; going through tunnels (closed and open at the exit end); and pausing in the down position on a low platform on command. Higher levels of competition also include such equipment as an open-sided crawl tunnel, weave poles,

The Shih Tzu's natural centerstage instincts combined with his enthusiasm make up for his size in agility competition. Little dogs can compete with Doberman-sized dogs and still fly to new heights. (Catherine A. Haake for Jo-an Condon)

and a sway bridge. The sport is exciting for the dogs, their handlers, and the spectators.

While the commands used in agility can vary, you should be consistent once you have chosen them so that the dog will not become confused. Give your commands early, so that the dog will be able to anticipate what he is to do next. There are three types of agility commands. Control commands are: "sit," "down," "wait," "easy," "here," "go," "right," and "left." Attention commands are the dog's name and "here." Action commands are: "climb," "jump." "over," "tunnel," "walk," and "weave."

Begin with an energetic warm-up, encouraging your dog with play and toys. Bait can be anything your dog likes to eat. Use small pieces, so that your dog can swallow the bait without chewing. While bait, toys, and whistles are permitted in training, they cannot be used in actual competition. When beginning agility training with a puppy, use poles on the ground rather than regular jumps. Use a buckle or breakaway collar in agility, never a choke or prong collar. The collar should not have any tags or other attachments that could become caught in the equipment. Be sure to keep your Shih Tzu's nails short and the hair between the pads of its feet trimmed so that the dog will have good footing. Your body movements are more important than verbal commands in signaling your dog; hand signals should be made with the hand closest to the dog.

Targeting is very important in agility training. There are three targeting commands: "look," "get it," and "go." The object of targeting is to teach your dog to focus on the handler and the exercise. The target can be a small white cloth or plastic lid. Praise and play are very important. The most difficult exercise to teach—the weave poles—is the only exception to the caution against frequent drilling and should be practiced often.

Many localities have agility clubs where you can train with your dog. One of the best ways to convince your dog (especially a young puppy, who will enjoy playing "follow the leader") that agility is fun is to take him to a class and let him watch how excited and self-assured the other dogs are. It's amazing how much a dog can learn about agility simply by observing.

The real key to teaching a Shih Tzu to enjoy agility is to capitalize on his desire to please you and make you laugh. If he sees that by doing something simple he can get you really excited, he'll be delighted. If he finds that each time he does this, he can also get his favorite treat, he'll be really enthusiastic. If, along the way, he decides that that see-saw wasn't as good an idea as it appeared at first, take many steps back to his initial achievements, reminding him how excited his success at the earlier level still makes you. If you have a trainer who has an understanding of what motivates a Shih Tzu (which is totally different from what inspires a classic agility dog such as a border collie), this is all to the good. If not, try to find a trainer who is willing to learn about different types of dogs.

A free copy of the *Regulations for Agility Trials* and a list of AKC clubs offering agility competition is available by phoning the AKC at 919-233-3600 or writing to the AKC Customer Service Department at 5580 Centerview Drive, Raleigh, NC 27606-0643. You can

Use a spotter on the other side of the teeter-totter. Move your dog slowly and have him wait at the top of the apparatus so that he comes to understand that his weight controls its movement. (Phyllis Celmer)

The weave poles are the most difficult exercise to teach. It is helpful to initially place exercise pens on either side of the poles so that your dog will learn to negotiate them as a single obstacle. (Phyllis Celmer)

Often the hardest thing about the platform is convincing your Shih Tzu, through words and body language, to stay there until you release him. He's been hurtling his little body around the course and is anxious to continue on to the next apparatus! (Kathy's Portraits for Michael Shea-Zackin)

build your own at-home practice course inexpensively, using such readily available items as PVC pipe, irrigation tubing, and painted lumber braced with cinder blocks.

Once you have been training for a while, enter an agility match, or enter a regular trial for exhibition only (you will not be compet-ing for prizes or titles). You don't have to wait until your dog is letter-perfect. After all, this is supposed to be fun, and entering trials even when your dog isn't ready is a great way to pinpoint problem areas (yours and your dog's) before entering formal competition.

Agility tunnels are both open- and closed-ended. When teaching your Shih Tzu to negotiate the closed tunnel, initially hold the closed end open so your dog can see you. (Phyllis Celmer)

JUNIOR SHOWMANSHIP

Unlike conformation competition, in which the dogs are judged, junior showmanship evaluates the skill of the young handler. Junior showmanship began in the New York area in 1933 and was recognized by the American Kennel Club in 1971, when the rules were standardized. The object of junior showmanship is to teach young people good sportsmanship and handling skills and to help them learn about dogs and dog shows.

Junior showmanship competition, offered at most all-breed shows and some specialty shows, is open to children between the ages of 10 and 18. The junior handler must gait his or her dog with the others around the ring and have it stand for examination by the judge and gait individually. The dog must be owned or co-owned by the junior handler or a member of his immediate family and must also be entered and shown in breed or obedience at the same show.

If you think your child might want to participate in junior showmanship, go to a dog show and watch the classes and talk about junior showmanship with the young handlers there. Many dog clubs offer handling classes where your child can practice handling skills. You can obtain a free copy of the *Rules and Regulations for Junior Showmanship* and a geographical list of dog clubs from the AKC, 5580 Centerview Drive, Raleigh, NC 27606.

CANINE FREESTYLE

This is a very new sport that expands the sport of obedience by including music and choreography. It is based on a similar sport for horses known as dressage. The international Canine Freestyle Federation has of-

If your child enjoys dogs and dog shows, you may want to encourage him or her to become involved in Junior Showmanship competition.

fered competitions in this sport since 1997. For more information, contact the CFF at 21900 Foxden Lane, Leesburg, VA 20175. The CFF home page is http://home.sprynet.com/sprynet/k9trainer/homepage.htm.

THERAPY AND THE CANINE GOOD CITIZENSHIP TEST

Many Shih Tzu and their owners have found great satisfaction working in pet therapy. Pet therapy dogs (large and small) visit patients in medical facilities and other institutions who can benefit from interacting with dogs. The results are often remarkable. Therapy dogs are also used to educate young children, including those in 4-H and scouting groups, about responsible dog ownership.

A therapy dog is happy and confident. Most facilities require that a therapy dog pass the AKC's Canine Good Citizenship (CGC) test, which indicates that the dog is well mannered and interacts well with people and other dogs. To pass the test, your Shih Tzu must be able to accept a friendly stranger, sit politely for petting, allow itself to be examined and groomed, walk under your control without straining on the leash (even when passing through a group of people), "sit" or "down" and "stay" on command, come when called, behave politely around other dogs, remain confident in the face of common distractions, and allow itself to be held on the lead by another person while you walk away without becoming unduly agitated. Many pet superstores offer CGC training as a service to the community, or contact the AKC.

For more information about therapy programs, contact Therapy Dogs International, 6 Hilltop Road, Mendham, NJ 07945, one of the other therapy associations (such as the Delta Society), or an individual already involved in canine therapy in your community. In order to be qualified as a therapy dog by Therapy Dogs International, your Shih Tzu must earn a TDI title. This requires a CGC award plus other exercises. A small dog like a Shih Tzu, for example, must allow strangers to pick it up and not show fright of wheelchairs, walkers, or canes. It is impor-

Shih Tzu can make spectacular therapy dogs. Their loving, outgoing personalities brighten the days of many nursing home residents and hospital patients. (Phyllis Celmer)

Therapy dogs can be large or small. Because Shih Tzu are cute, happy, and friendly, they make excellent candidates for this ministry. (Phyllis Celmer)

One of the great joys of rescue work is finding loving homes like this one for Shih Tzu abandoned by their former owners. (Phyllis Celmer)

These dogs, shown with their new owners, were among a group of more than 50 filthy, sick, and matted Shih Tzu rescued by a group of dedicated volunteers. Thanks to the people who were willing to open their hearts and homes to these dogs, they now enjoy a very different life! (Phyllis Celmer)

tant that a therapy dog have a calm, even temperament; it should not be so aloof that it makes patients feel rejected nor so energetic that it could cause fright or injury.

As you know, just being near your Shih Tzu makes you feel good. Because he has given you so much, why not let him share his love with others in need?

BREED RESCUE

Involvement in Shih Tzu rescue is another extremely rewarding activity. Contact the ASTC or your local Shih Tzu club to find out how you can help. If you do not have the facilities to provide a temporary foster home for a rescue dog, you can still look for Shih Tzu at your local animal shelter, tend to the phone, provide transportation to the vet, groom, or otherwise contribute to local rescue efforts. At the very least, keep the names and telephone numbers of local Shih Tzu rescue contacts by your telephone so that you can tell them if you hear of a Shih Tzu in need of a new home or a person willing to adopt a rescue dog. If you breed your Shih Tzu, be responsible, so that you do not contribute to the rescue problem.

The Health of the Shih Tzu

S ome of the basics involved in having a healthy Shih Tzu are part of the regular grooming process, such as routine eye, ear, foot, and anal gland care and flea and tick checks and treatment. You should take your new puppy to the vet promptly to ensure that it is healthy, and you should be able to return it to the breeder if it has any health problems you are unwilling to live with.

If your Shih Tzu has diarrhea or vomits just once, don't be too concerned. Puppies, particularly, tend to put anything and everything into their mouths and get rid of what doesn't set right promptly. If your dog has repeated bouts of diarrhea or vomiting; appears lethargic; goes off its food (except when teething); suffers from recurrent lameness, seizures, or depression; and/or is running a fever (a normal temperature for a dog is 100 to 102 degrees F), have it checked by your veterinarian. Take your dog's temperature with a rectal thermometer that has been dipped in a lubricating jelly.

INOCULATIONS AND ROUTINE CHECKUPS

An inoculation record should accompany your new Shih Tzu. Many breeders prefer to give "puppy shots" (distemper, hepatitis, parainfluenza, parvovirus and corona virus) at 8, 12, and 16 weeks (or 6, 9, 12, and 16 weeks) of age, with a booster due once a year thereafter. Do not add leptospirosis to the vaccine mix until 12 weeks of age, as this can greatly increase the chances of developing autoimmune diseases. The first rabies shot is usually given at six months, although some states require this as early as three months. Booster shots should be administered thereafter as your vet recommends. There could be other vaccinations given as well, such as for Lyme disease, depending upon what problems are found in your area. In most parts of the country, heartworm preventative tablets are given in a dosage determined by weight during mosquito season (which may be all year 'round in the Deep South). The monthly pills are safer and as effective as the daily ones. Some pills also kill roundworms, hookworms, and whipworms, which can be helpful if your dog has an internal-parasite problem. Your puppy will not need a blood test to be given heartworm medication the first time if he is less than six months old, but he will need to have his blood checked each spring thereafter before you can have your prescription renewed. Please discuss all vaccinations given and the schedule for booster shots with your breeder and your veterinarian. The health record will also indicate when your puppy was tested for parasites and if and when it was wormed. Thereafter, take a stool sample in to be checked by your veterinarian annually or if symptoms warrant. Your annual visit for booster shots and a fecal sample will give your veterinarian an opportunity to examine your Shih Tzu thoroughly on a regular basis.

Some states require that a health certificate signed by a veterinarian indicating that a puppy has received the required inoculations and been checked for parasites accompany every puppy when it is sold.

Generally, Shih Tzu are very long-lived dogs with few health problems, and responsible breeders are doing all that they can to ensure that this remains true. Even though the odds are against your dog ever demonstrating the symptoms of any serious emergency problems,

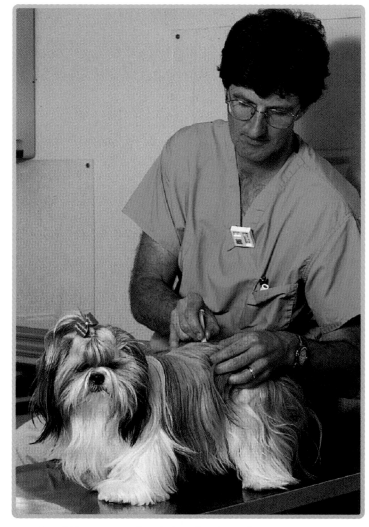

Your breeder and/or veterinarian will recommend the appropriate inoculation schedule for your Shih Tzu. Present a health record from the breeder to your veterinarian upon your first visit. (Isabelle Francais)

you should be aware of and alert for them for the sake of your dog and the future welfare of the breed.

EMERGENCY FIRST AID

Often we know there is something wrong with our pet's health or condition but we cannot identify what it is or its cause. The *Dog Owner's Home Veterinary Handbook* is a practical guide written for the layman which covers a wide variety of signs and symptoms of illness and disease. The first chapter is dedicated to emergencies. Such a book is a wise investment that could save you time and money when attempting to identify your Shih Tzu's health problem in order to discuss it with your veterinarian. It

could save your pet's life in an emergency, although it is *not* a substitute for veterinary consultation and care. Be sure that you feel comfortable with the veterinarian you select (local breeders may be able to recommend one familiar with Shih Tzu). Your vet should be on call 24 hours a day or have links to a 24-hour emergency service.

You should assemble a basic "doggy first-aid kit" and keep it in your home and take it with you when you travel with your pet. This kit should include cotton, gauze pads and rolls, adhesive tape, cotton swabs, tweezers, scissors, a thermometer, 3% hydrogen peroxide, antihistamine, antidiarrheal, neosporin antibiotic ointment (for ear infections and hot spots), antibiotic eye drops or ointment, a general antibiotic ointment, charcoal suspension, milk of magnesia, a product containing diamenhydrinate (preventing nausea and motion sickness), and baby aspirin. There may be other items you would like to add, depending on your dog and whether it has any specific health problems.

POISONING

If you suspect that your Shih Tzu has ingested a poisonous substance, prompt treatment may be needed to save his life. Try to determine just what your pet has eaten. If his symptoms (which may include vomiting, abdominal pain, cramps, tremors, convulsions, diarrhea, a swollen tongue or mouth, and central nervous system involvement) are caused by acids, alkalis, solvents, heavy-duty cleaners, petroleum products, tranquilizers, or sharp objects; if he is extremely depressed or comatose; or if he swallowed the poison more than two hours ago, do not induce vomiting. Otherwise, you can try to get him to expel the poison by giving him three doses (at ten-minute intervals) of a teaspoon of 3% hydrogen peroxide, or by placing one-half teaspoon of salt on the back of his tongue. Among the common causes of poisoning in dogs are acetaminophen, ibuprofen, chocolate, antifreeze, insecticides, and a number of household plants (including dieffenbachia and philodendron). In case of poisoning, the number for the 24-hour nationwide veterinary poison control hotline (NAPCC) is 1-900-680-000 (there is a charge for calls to NAPCC). It is best to have your veterinarian call for you, although calls from pet owners are accepted.

BREATHING PROBLEMS AND HEAT STROKE

The Shih Tzu is a brachycephalic (short-faced) breed. Many Shih Tzu puppies, especially those with very short noses, have slightly pinched nostrils, particularly when they are teething. They may snort and snuffle, snore, and have a watery, clear nasal discharge. (A thick, yellow or green discharge indicates a respiratory infection; you should see your vet and have this treated with appropriate antibiotics.) This problem generally clears up with age. If your Shih Tzu's nostrils are so pinched that it can breathe only through its mouth and has difficulty eating, even after it has cut its adult teeth, you may want to have it checked by a specialist to see if it needs to have its nostrils surgically opened or its tonsils removed to help open the airway. Some Shih Tzu have elongated soft palates that periodically obstruct the airway and cause the dog to gasp for air. Such palates may require surgical shortening if attacks are frequent and prolonged. (Almost every Shih Tzu does this once in a while when overly excited; you can put your finger over the dog's nose to force him to breathe through his mouth, which will cause the palate to drop back into its normal position.) Again, give breathing problems time so long as your dog is thriving. Many veterinarians unfamiliar with our breed are far too quick to recommend corrective surgery. If your Shih Tzu does have breathing difficulties, such as labored breathing when physically or emotionally stressed and a dry, honking cough, often accompanied by gagging, there are some things you can do short of surgery to relieve his discomfort. Restrict physical activities during the hottest part of the day, use a harness instead of a collar or lead to avoid external pressure on the airways, and do not allow your dog to become overweight. Bronchodilators, corticosteroids, and cough suppressants may relieve the symptoms associated with an elongated soft palate, although they will not cure the condition.

Your Shih Tzu's short face also makes it very prone to heat stroke. Be sure never to leave your Shih Tzu in a car with the windows closed in hot weather. Your car can become like an oven in only the few short minutes it takes to run an errand. Also be sure not to take your dog for long walks in the hottest part of the day. Not only can your dog become overheated, but a hot road can burn the pads of his feet. Freezer ice packs and plenty of water are necessities when traveling with your Shih Tzu in hot weather.

If your dog evidences signs of heat stroke—rapid, noisy, frantic breathing; a bright red tongue that curls upward and bright red mucous membranes; thick saliva; possibly vomiting; and a very high rectal temperature—you must do everything you can to cool him down at once or he may die. If his temperature is less than 104 degrees F, move him to cooler surroundings. If it is higher, put him in a tub of cool water. Once you have brought his temperature down, take him to your vet to be sure he does not need additional treatment. Any temperature of more than 106 degrees F requires immediate veterinary intervention.

EYES, EARS, AND TEETH

The Shih Tzu has large eyes in shallow sockets that may be easily injured. Be sure to check daily for redness, tearing, squinting, or other signs of irritation. If you notice any problem, *see your veterinarian immediately* so that the damage does not worsen or result in permanent blindness.

Corneal ulcers, which look like small dots in the dark part of the eye, can be caused by foreign objects such as grass seeds, by careless grooming, and by scratches. They can be treated with medication if caught early but may require surgery if not attended to promptly.

A blow to the head or pulling back the skin on the head too tightly when grooming may force the eye out of its socket, requiring veterinary treatment within minutes to save vision and the eye.

Several hereditary eye disorders, or disorders suspected to be hereditary, occasionally occur in Shih Tzu. The dog may be unable to close its eyelid properly over the cornea, leading to inflammation, ulceration, or scarring of the cornea. There may be eyelashes abnormally located in the eyelid margin or emerging through the eyelid conjuctiva; these are very painful and can lead to ulcers and blindness. Dry eye, an abnormality of the tear film characterized by a thick, yellow discharge,

Because the Shih Tzu's eyes are easily injured, daily inspections are recommended. (Isabelle Francais)

leads to ulceration and vision loss unless treated daily with corrective eyedrops.

Hereditary or juvenile cataracts and progressive retinal atrophy (PRA) have been reported in Shih Tzu. These diseases lead to blindness; dogs with these conditions should never be bred. Because these diseases may not be evident immediately, annual eye examinations are recommended, particularly for breeding stock.

Because Shih Tzu have drop ears, there is little air circulation in the ear canal, promoting disease. Watch to be sure your dog has no dark, yeasty, or odorous discharge when you clean its ears, and check its ears if it is constantly rubbing or scratching at them. Sometimes the first sign of ear problems is a "different" odor from the ear. Many vets recommend keeping the hair pulled from inside the ear canal for better air circulation, although others feel that leaving the hair inside the ear helps to wick moisture to the outside and keeps water from entering the ear canal during bathing. Clean the ears periodically with a canine ear-wash solution. You can saturate small cotton balls with ear wash, place them inside the upper earwells, and massage the ears gently to loosen the debris inside the ear. Then use a dry cotton ball to finish cleaning the ears. Do not poke deep into the ear canal with a cotton swab or other instrument; you could puncture your dog's eardrum.

It is important to clean your dog's teeth regularly and to watch for signs of dental problems, such as soft gums, loose teeth, and bad breath, so that they can be treated early. The Shih Tzu is generally undershot (its upper jaw is shorter than its lower one), which alters the standard chewing and biting pattern. Also, missing and misaligned teeth are common in our breed. Baby teeth may not fall out when the permanent teeth emerge. It is especially important to keep a careful eye on retained baby teeth in a show puppy, as they may cause the permanent teeth to become misaligned if they are not removed.

Check for fleas and other possible coat and skin irritations during your daily brushing session. (Isabelle Francais)

ALLERGIES AND SKIN PROBLEMS

Your Shih Tzu, just like virtually any other dog, can suffer from fungal or bacteriological infections of the skin. Be alert for any skin irritation during regular grooming (especially raw or reddened areas under the eyes, on the stomach, and around the mouth) and apply an antibiotic ointment to the affected area. If the irritation does not clear up shortly, see your veterinarian. Your Shih Tzu may also develop small fluid-filled cysts or infected hair follicles. These generally must be expressed when ready to rupture and medicated to avoid secondary infections.

Many skin problems in Shih Tzu are related to flea allergies, so be sure to keep your dog and its environment as pest-free as possible. A few Shih Tzu may have allergic reactions to certain foods, insecticides, shampoos, or pollens. Diagnosing such allergies may be a long and expensive process.

If allergies to dogs are a problem for a member of your family, the allergy sufferer may not be allergic to Shih Tzu. Our breed has hair instead of fur, like poodles and several other breeds, which means that Shih Tzu do not cause allergic reactions in people sensitive to fur. If you are allergic to animal dander, there are special products that can be applied to your dog to lessen such allergic reactions.

HERNIAS AND UNDESCENDED TESTICLES

Small umbilical (belly button) hernias are quite common in Shih Tzu puppies. If the opening is small, with only a fat pad (no intestine) protruding, it will likely close by itself as the puppy matures. As with slightly pinched nostrils, many vets unfamiliar with our breed are much too quick to recommend corrective surgery. Unless there is danger that the intestine will become strangulated in the hernia, wait until the dog is mature before making a decision about whether surgery is needed. If your pet is being spayed or neutered, this is a good time to correct a hernia. A hernia in a bitch should always be closed before she is bred because of the risks associated with increased abdominal weight during pregnancy.

Inguinal (groin) hernias are more dangerous and more likely to require surgical repair. Because there is a likelihood that such hernias are hereditary, a dog with an inguinal hernia should not be bred. Also, the AKC considers dogs who have had surgery for inguinal hernias to have altered their appearance; dogs having had such surgery cannot be shown.

A male Shih Tzu should have both testicles normally descended into the scrotum. A young puppy may "pull up" one or both testicles when nervous or cold, but both testicles should be down by the time the puppy is mature. Your Shih Tzu cannot be shown in conformation if both testicles are not descended and should not be bred. If one or both testicles are not descended by the age of six months, the dog should be neutered. This will involve an abdominal incision to remove the retained testicle(s). It is more expensive than a regular neuter but must be done, as there is a *greatly* increased risk of cancer in a retained testicle.

OPEN FONTANELLES

A soft spot in the skull that does not close by the age of six months is called an open fontanelle. It is often blamed for seizures in puppies; however, its actual significance is unknown. Many dogs with open fontanelles can live normal lives. However, they are *much* more prone to injury, and even a light blow to the head may kill them.

IMMUNE-RELATED PROBLEMS

The Shih Tzu is one of many breeds sometimes affected by immune-related problems. Any Shih Tzu exhibiting signs of thyroid malfunction, such as hair loss, waxy and smelly ears, a greasy itchy skin that may develop patches of black pigment, lethargy, obesity, and irregular heat cycles should have its blood tested for thyroid function after a blood count, blood chemistry panel, and urinalysis have been performed. Pets exhibiting symptoms of thyroid malfunction should have FT_4D and cTSH tests. Breeding aminals should have these tests, plus either TgAA or T_3aa and T_4aa, to provide a more complete picture of thyroid function; if results are normal but clinical signs of hypothyroidism persist, the tests should be repeated in two to six months. Medication to correct thyroid malfunction is available but, once started, it must continue for the rest of the dog's life, so it is important that the diagnosis be accurate.

Another immune-mediated disease occasionally seen in Shih Tzu is von Willebrand's disease, a blood-clotting deficiency. Your veterinarian should therefore perform a toenail trimming test for clotting function before surgery. Breeding stock may be tested for von Willebrand's disease; it is extremely important that the blood for this test be drawn properly.

JOINT AND SPINAL PROBLEMS

While Shih Tzu are small dogs, and thus can generally walk normally even with unsound joints, it is important to x-ray the hips and shoulders of any Shih Tzu who will be jumping in obedience or agility competition. If there is a problem, you do not want to harm your dog by having him jump when he is not physically able. Shih Tzu find jumping fun and will keep on trying to please even when it hurts or possibly injures them. Breeding stock should have hips certified by the Orthopedic Foundation for Animals (OFA) after two years of age to avoid passing dysplastic hips along to their offspring.

Another joint problem found in Shih Tzu are luxating patellas (kneecaps). Shih Tzu with this problem may have inherited it or acquired it by injury. It is caused by a too shallow groove in the part of the femur where the kneecap fits, weak ligaments, or misalignment of the tendons and muscles that hold the kneecap in place. The kneecap can be pushed in and out of position or slip out of position by itself, at which time the dog may pick up the affected leg for a few steps and stretch it to put the kneecap back in place. A severely affected dog may limp and suffer pain. Dogs with luxating patellas should not be bred; the condition can and should be corrected by surgery in severely affected dogs.

On extremely rare occasions, one or more of the spinal disks of a Shih Tzu (particularly one that is older, obese, and very long in back) may deteriorate. Sometimes the dog will recover with cortisone treatments; sometimes it will become paralyzed in the rear and be unable to walk. If your Shih Tzu is having difficulty standing, climbing stairs, or jumping on the couch, or if it seems in pain when touched or lifted, contact your veterinarian.

To avoid injuring the bones and joints of your puppy, feed him a well-balanced diet, give him secure footing, do not allow him to become overweight or encourage him to walk on his hind legs, and never pick him up by his legs (put your hands around his chest instead). In an area where Lyme disease is common, be sure to have your Shih Tzu tested for this disease if he begins limping for no apparent reason and evidences no signs of tenderness in any specific area. An older Shih Tzu, like most older dogs of any breed, may suffer from arthritis.

KIDNEY AND BLADDER STONES

If your dog stops urinating, has blood in its urine, or clearly is in pain when voiding, it may have kidney or bladder stones. Surgery is generally used to remove large stones, while smaller ones can sometimes be dissolved by changing the dog's diet. Any dog that has had kidney or bladder stones should be put on a special diet to keep more stones from forming. Because such symptoms can be life-threatening, and because they may also be caused by infections or other kinds of obstructions, it is important to seek prompt veterinary attention.

RENAL DYSPLASIA

Renal dysplasia is perhaps the most common and serious hereditary problem in our breed. In this disease, the kidney fails to develop normally. A severely affected dog will vomit periodically, fail to thrive, drink excessive water, and have extremely dilute urine. It will generally die at a young age. If you suspect your dog may have renal dysplasia, urine specific gravity, BUN, and creatinine tests will substantiate your suspicions in a dog with very little remaining kidney function. An ultrasound scan of the kidney may show scarring and other findings typical of the disease in some moderately affected Shih Tzu, but the only definitive test to locate slightly affected dogs at the present

time is a wide-wedge biopsy of the kidney (a surgical procedure).

The problem with this disease is that many dogs are only slightly affected, with no clinical symptoms, and may live out normal life spans and pass the disease on, in varying degrees, to their offspring.

Losing a Shih Tzu to renal dysplasia is heartbreaking. For this reason, the ASTC is sponsoring research into locating a genetic marker for renal dysplasia. Once this marker is located the presence or absence of the disease can be determined by DNA testing of a cheek swab. At that time *there will be no excuse not to test, and all breeding animals should be tested.*

To further this research, we need cheek swab samples from Shih Tzu known to have renal dysplasia or to have produced the disease as determined by wide wedge kidney biopsy. If you own such a dog (samples need not be from related dogs and can be collected by the owner) and are willing to provide cheek swab samples, please contact the ASTC research project coordinator at 1829 F & S Grade Road, Sedro Wooley, WA 98284-9664 for swabs and procedures. Your identity and that of your dog will remain confidential and you will have the reward of doing something to benefit your breed. You can obtain a free pamphlet telling you more about this disease from the ASTC secretary.

PORTAL SYSTEMIC SHUNT

Portal systemic shunt, or canine portal caval shunt, is a rare disease of the liver occasionally found in Shih Tzu and a number of other breeds. It is usually diagnosed in puppies less than one year of age who are stunted, thin, and depressed and may exhibit various signs of central nervous system disorders such as blindness, circling, head pressing, and seizures. Affected puppies may vomit and drink and urinate excessively, and a urine sediment may reveal ammonium biurate crystals characteristic of the disease. The disease in small dogs is caused by a shunt outside the liver that diverts blood around

Attending to your Shih Tzu's health needs ensures him the long life he was bred to live—from his toes to his teeth. Generally our breed is a hardy, problem-free companion who thrives on your caring and attention. (Isabelle Francais)

the liver. This prevents the blood from being detoxified by the liver. Surgery to close the shunt is difficult and often unsuccessful, but dogs not receiving surgery will inevitably die from the disease.

SPAYING AND NEUTERING

The ASTC recommends the spaying and neutering of all pet Shih Tzu to help control the pet overpopulation problem and eliminate the risk of unwanted pregnancy, messy heat cycles, hormone-related cancer, and male leg-lifting and roaming. Such surgery will not affect the health or temperament of your pet.

CARING FOR THE OLDER SHIH TZU

Most Shih Tzu begin to show signs of age at about twelve. Their vision and hearing may deteriorate, their joints may stiffen, and they may become less active. They may have to eliminate more frequently due to old-age kidney problems and become less tolerant of young children or rough play. Be sure to give your elder dog plenty of love and frequent health checkups. If you see signs such as labored breathing, weakness, loss of appetite, coughing or wheezing, and a watery swelling of the abdomen in a Shih Tzu of any age, be sure your vet checks for signs of heart abnormalities.

Prompt medical attention can often add years to an elderly dog's life, and the acquisition of a new puppy can sometimes make an old dog act young again. Just be sure, if you introduce a new companion, that you give your faithful friend extra love—your puppy grew up with his littermates, while your older dog has been used to being the center of attention.

Breeding Your Shih Tzu (or Not)

You do not have to breed your Shih Tzu to be a Shih Tzu fancier. Most people are happy to purchase their Shih Tzu, love them, and leave breeding to others. Most purebred AKC registered dogs should not be bred because they have structural, temperament, or health problems that should not be perpetuated. They may make wonderful pets, but the goal of breeding should always be to produce puppies that are of better quality than the parents. To do this, you must learn to recognize a quality dog when you see it, be able to honestly evaluate your dog's faults and virtues, know what improvements you wish to make, and genuinely try to leave the Shih Tzu breed you love a little better than you found it. Remember that breeding almost never results in a financial profit, even excluding your time investment, and that it costs no more to raise a good-quality dog than a poor one.

There is no excuse for an accidental litter—if you own an unspayed bitch, watch carefully so that you know when she comes in season and keep her confined for the entire time she is in heat. Better yet, have her spayed if you do not intend to breed her. Selecting a stud dog or a brood bitch requires a great deal of knowledge and careful thought. Both should be of good quality and in good physical condition and not have any serious faults. A dog that is shy, unstable, or nasty can pass on such a temperament to its puppies, which will then not even be suitable pets. You should also evaluate your own qualifications to be a Shih Tzu breeder.

ARE YOU PREPARED TO BE A RESPONSIBLE BREEDER?

As a responsible breeder, you should be well educated about Shih Tzu and be prepared to offer specific information about Shih Tzu in general and about your dogs specifically. Your breeding stock should be healthy, mentally sound, and be able to be seen by visitors. You should maintain the highest standards of cleanliness, care, and canine health. You should screen for genetic defects before breeding, and all of your breeding stock should have appropriate registry certification numbers and should have all blood tests necessary for heritable-defect screening. You should encourage the buyers of your puppies to keep up these screening procedures throughout their new pets' lives.

A responsible breeder provides a sales agreement with each puppy sold; keeps good records (pedigrees, registration, and health) of all his/her dogs. The American Kennel Club requires that you keep accurate records of all your dog activities. To find out more about these record-keeping requirements, write to the AKC for the pamphlet *Rules Applying to Registration and Dog Shows*.

Before selling a puppy, a responsible breeder questions a prospective buyer about family situation, job schedule, previous dog-owning experience, etc. Remember, creating a life should mean that you will be responsible for your puppy for the rest of its days. Do not sell a dog to someone simply because they have enough money. Will this person be willing to devote the necessary time to training and coat care? Is the personality of a particular puppy suited to the lifestyle of the would-be owner? If in doubt, you may want to visit the prospective buyer's home and check with other breeders in the area.

As the goal of breeding should be to produce puppies that are better than their parents, breed only Shih Tzu that are good representatives of the breed standard and have been tested for inheritable diseases. (Earl Takahashi)

This stud dog is pictured with several offspring out of different bitches. When selecting a stud dog, try to choose one that is prepotent for the attributes you feel are most important for a mating with your particular bitch. (Tammarie Larson)

When problems occur, the responsible breeder is open about them, because genetic problems cannot be removed from our breed without the help of each and every Shih Tzu breeder. The responsible breeder is knowledgeable enough about our breed to answer a puppy buyer's many questions and provide resources and information.

GENETIC TESTING

The ASTC strongly recommends that genetic testing for known hereditary health problems be done *before* you even consider using your Shih Tzu for breeding. Consultation with your veterinarian is also recommended. No reliable means of genetic testing is currently available for umbilical hernia, inguinal hernia, portal systemic shunt (PSS), or autoimmune hemolytic anemia.

Eyes should be tested yearly for the following known problems:

Progressive Retinal Atrophy (PRA) and **juvenile cataracts,** both tested by ERG or direct opthalmoscope, and **entropion** (inverted lashes). Eye tests should be registered with the Canine Eye Registry Founda-tion (CERF), SCC - A, Purdue University, Lafayette, IN 47907. Phone (317) 494-8179.

Renal dysplasia (an inherited developmental defect of the kidney in Shih Tzu) may be suspected due to unsatisfactory results in urine specific gravity and urine concentration tests. If the urine is very dilute, indicating that the dog's kidneys are not functioning properly, BUN and creatinine blood tests may be performed. Note, however, that BUN and creatinine tests in the normal range mean only that the dog has at least 30% kidney function, not that it is free of renal dysplasia. An ultrasound examination of the kidney may spot characteristic signs of renal dysplasia in severely and some moderately affected dogs, although it will not pick up slightly affected dogs that may pass the disease on to their offspring. The only definitive method to date to determine specifically whether abnormal kidney function is due to renal dysplasia is a surgical wide wedge biopsy of the kidney, although research into finding a genetic marker for the disease so that its presence or absence may be determined by a noninvasive test is being conducted.

The presence or absence of **hip dysplasia** can be determined by x-ray. A dog cannot be OFA-certified for normal hips until after two years of age, although preliminary x-rays may be done at an earlier age. For more information, contact the Orthopedic Foundation for Animals, 2300 Nifong Boulevard, Colombia, MO 65201. Phone (314) 442-0418.

Blood tests for **von Willebrand's disease** (a blood clotting disorder) and **thyroid disorders** may be sent to either Animal Health Diagnostic Lab, Michigan State University, PO Box 30076, East Lansing, MI 48824, or to P.A.L., 17672-A Cowan Avenue, Suite 200, Irving, CA 92714. Your veterinarian may also recommend a bile acid test before breeding.

THE STUD DOG

If you are thinking about using your Shih Tzu at stud, you should first be sure that he is a good representative of the breed in terms of health, temperament, and conformation. Your pet-quality male does not need to be bred for his health; in fact, he is likely to become territorial and begin lifting his leg in your house, making him a less desirable pet. If he is not of sufficient quality to do well in the show ring, he should not be bred, as the primary purpose of breeding is to improve the quality of the breed—not to produce more pet puppies.

Also, remember that as the owner of a stud dog, you always have the right to refuse to breed any female. Do not breed to unregistered or pet-quality bitches, or to any bitch owned by an individual you do not feel has the best interests of the breed (and the puppies out of your stud dog) at heart. Refusing to breed unsuitable dogs is one way to decrease the number of unwanted Shih Tzu, so do your part.

All genetic testing should be completed and current on your stud dog if you plan to breed him. You should also have genetic information on the dogs in his pedigree, to be sure that he will not be transmitting unwanted and possibly lethal genetic faults to his offspring.

Make sure that your stud dog is in good physical condition and has an annual health exam by a veterinarian, including a test for brucellosis (an incurable bacterial disease that is a major cause of reproductive failure and can be spread by sexual intercourse and contact with infected secretions). He must be free from external and internal parasites, and all inoculations should be current.

Do you have facilities for the secure and proper care of a visiting bitch? This includes having time to help her adjust to her temporary home. Remember that while she is with you, you must accept the responsibility for her welfare.

If you want to breed to get another Shih Tzu just like the one you have, it would be best to purchase another puppy. Breeding healthy quality puppies takes a lot of time and knowledge; you are unlikely to make money and you could even lose your bitch. (Tammarie Larson)

Do you have the skills and ability to handle the actual mating process (including artificial insemination, if necessary) and the knowledge to ensure that the breeding takes place at the optimum time to ensure pregnancy? You cannot simply turn the stud dog and brood bitch loose and expect them to do "what comes naturally." Not all bitches are cooperative, and one of the pair could be severely injured if they are left alone unsupervised.

Be sure you are able to answer specific questions about what your dog is producing—both the good and the bad. The objective is to find two excellent dogs that compliment each other, rather than two mediocre dogs or two that might produce the same fault if bred together.

Ask what the bitch has produced and to whom she was bred. If you have not seen the bitch, ask to see photographs and request information about possible health and temperament problems that she may exhibit or have produced. You want your mating to result in puppies that both you and the bitch owner will be proud of, offspring that will not create problems for their owners.

Require the bitch to have the same genetic tests that you have on your stud dog. Keep a three- or four-generation pedigree of every bitch your dog has been bred to; include genetic testing on those dogs in that pedigree. In this way, if problems do arise in the offspring, you will be better able to trace them to the source and avoid repeating your mistakes.

Have a complete and *specific* stud contract with a place to include exceptions. Both parties should have a signed copy. This contract should specify, among other things, what happens if the breeding does not take (generally, the bitch owner is entitled to a free return stud service); what the stud fee is and when it is payable (generally at the time of mating); what happens if the stud fee is a puppy and there is only one puppy; and what happens if all of the puppies die.

Inquire into the selling practices of the owner of the brood bitch, conducting as careful an interview as you would with a prospective buyer of one of your puppies. You have a responsibility to the breed and to your stud dog to do all that you can to ensure that his puppies do not wind up in shelters or on the street, and that the owner of the bitch feels a responsibility to his/her puppies for the rest of their lives. You may want to specify in your stud-service contract that puppies resulting from the breeding will not knowingly be sold for resale.

Keep accurate records of the times and dates of breedings, keeping the owner of the bitch informed. Send a written record of the dates of breedings to the owner of the bitch.

When returning the bitch, include a copy of your stud's pedigree with all of the genetic testing that has been done noted on it.

Make sure both parties agree as to when the AKC papers are to be signed, and whether pet puppies are to be sold under spay/neuter contracts and/or limited registration.

THE BROOD BITCH

The owner of the female makes the decision to breed and selects the stud dog to use. Raising healthy well-adjusted puppies is rewarding, but it is also very time-consuming. Before you decide to breed your bitch, there are many things to consider.

First, be sure that she is of good quality and does not have any serious faults. If she has a major fault or is unsound, mentally or physically, she should never be bred. A poorly bred Shih Tzu is unlikely to produce quality puppies, or even her own likeness. If all you really want is another Shih Tzu just like your pet, you would be better off purchasing one rather than becoming responsible for puppies that might be turn out to be sickly, unattractive, or antisocial. If things go wrong during whelping, and they certainly can (especially if you are not knowledgeable), you could wind up losing not only your puppies but also your bitch.

Because a quality-producing bitch is the foundation of many a noted breeding program, it is unlikely that a bitch already proven to be a producer of quality puppies will ever be offered for sale. The best the seeker can do is to purchase a well-bred

Breeding requires both money and time. Two mothers with their litters are socializing with a visiting aunt. It is interesting to note that the first Shih Tzu litter produced from frozen semen was whelped in 1998, seven years after the death of the sire, by surgically inserting two vials of semen into the dam. (Maureen Clough)

puppy out of such a producer and hope that the puppy will turn out as well as or better than her dam. Good bitches, because they are so valuable, will have been very carefully bred for generations, and your puppy's pedigree should reflect that fact.

Breeding for the sake of educating your children is not a reason to have a litter. Suppose the litter arrives in the middle of the night (which is very common)? Suppose a puppy is deformed and must be put down, or is born dead? The bitch may well be screaming and trying to bite you while a puppy is being born, which is no way to introduce a child to the "joys of birth." Your bitch may not be a natural mother and may try to kill her puppies or refuse to nurse them. Breeding can be very satisfying emotionally, but you must be prepared for the possibility of tragedy.

Make sure you have the *finances and time* to be there for the whelping and complete care of the litter. Do you have proper facilities for the whelping and care of the puppies, especially if you are unable to sell them right away? Veteran breeders estimate that it takes more than 130 hours of real work to raise the average litter—at least two hours a day, every day. A Shih Tzu cannot be left alone to whelp and requires almost constant attention for several days thereafter. This means that you will have to take time off from your job and have many sleepless nights. Later, you will have to check the puppies regularly and socialize them properly, groom and train them, and, of course, clean the whelping box.

Interviewing prospective buyers also takes a great deal of time. The people who expressed their desire for one of your puppies often change their minds once the puppies are born, and it is hard for a novice breeder without a reputation and referrals to find suitable buyers. Pet puppies, in particular, become less salable as they grow older. What will you do if you cannot find good homes for your puppies? Will you become less careful in screening your buyers and agree to sell to less suitable owners? If so, what will be the fate of the babies you

Make sure all genetic testing has been completed on your bitch before deciding to breed her. Verify that the sire and dam of your bitch have also been checked for genetic anomalies. You do not want to perpetuate the genes for health problems.

Research several dogs that you feel would be suitable for your bitch, considering both pedigrees and genetic makeup. Discuss the possibility of breeding your bitch with the owner of the stud dog *well in advance.* Ask specific questions about the dog and what he has produced

Shih Tzu puppies are cute, but they are very curious and get into everything. Be sure you have enough time to care for them and socialize them properly before you decide to breed. (Edythe B. Kennedy)

brought into the world? Most veteran breeders do not breed unless they have advance cash deposits for an average-sized litter.

Breeding a litter is not a money-making proposition. It is very expensive to pay for health care, shots, stud fees, advertising, etc. This is even more true if your bitch has sick puppies or dies in whelp.

If you do decide to breed your bitch, realize that you have a lifetime responsibility for the Shih Tzu pups you've created. Screen prospective puppy buyers carefully, sell with spay and neuter contracts and/or limited registrations, and follow up after your puppies are sold. Responsible breeders should be willing to take back their puppies and find them new homes if any problems develop.

when bred to bitches with similar conformation and pedigrees.

Check on all requirements, stud service fees, shipping arrangements, stud service contract, etc. Stud service contracts are different with each stud dog owner; be sure you understand them.

Know how to tell when your female is ready to be bred. The receptive period on a bitch can vary by a week or more and can be long or short. Your vet can perform tests to give you a better idea of the correct breeding time if you are unsure.

Be sure all inoculations are current and that she is free of internal and external parasites and is in good physical condition. At the first sign of being in season, have a brucellosis test done and contact the owner of the stud dog.

Shih Tzu get along so well together that many people choose to own two. However, Shih Tzu require lots of individual attention. Do not become so enthusiastic that you wind up with more dogs than you can care for properly. (Earl Takahashi)

Whelping and Raising a Shih Tzu Litter

I f at all possible, you should arrange with an experienced Shih Tzu breeder to watch a whelping before you contemplate handling one on your own, and the assistance of such a person at your first whelping is invaluable. Many a puppy has died during birth because the dam's owner didn't know what to do.

Assuming that your mother-to-be is well fed and healthy, serious preparations for whelping should begin about 2 weeks before the "normal" due date of 63 days by introducing your bitch to her whelping box. There are many different styles of whelping boxes. You can purchase one, build one yourself from wood (sealed with varnish), or place a clean cardboard box inside a playpen. Commercial whelping boxes often have a railing around the inside high enough for a puppy to fit under it but low enough to keep the mother from accidentally smothering a puppy caught between her back and the side of the whelping box. For the first few days, the mother may be confused and "lose" such a puppy, which may be too small or too weak to escape.

In any case, the whelping area should be divided into a sleeping area for the bitch and her puppies and a larger area where the mother can escape from her babies to eat and eliminate and to get some much-needed rest and peace from time to time. The two areas should be divided by a low barrier (about 4 inches high) that will keep the babies on one side while allowing the mother to exit comfortably. This barrier can be raised as the puppies mature.

The whelping box should be placed in a quiet, warm, and draft-free area (Cold is the leading cause of death in young puppies, who are unable to regulate their own body temperature in the early days of their lives.) The bitch should be fed in this area and allowed to sleep there. If she considers this her place, she is less likely to try and have her puppies under the bed or behind a chair!

APPROACHING LABOR

Shih Tzu most often whelp early rather than late—56 days is quite common—so have all of your equipment assembled in plenty of time. You will need some old, soft, clean towels, scissors and surgical clamps (scissors-style with locking handles), alcohol for sterilizing the above, unwaxed dental floss and styptic powder for dealing with umbilical cords, and a jar of honey and a spoon.

A few days before whelping, the puppies generally drop. The bitch with the former watermelon silhouette changes shape, becoming thin above while carrying around a "basketball" below. There are many signs of imminent whelping, including vigorous scratching at the bedding or in corners, refusal to eat, loose stool, and a glassy-eyed, preoccupied look; but keep in mind that all or none of these signs can occur the day of or several days before whelping. Take the bitch's temperature rectally twice daily from about the 55th day; whelping will almost always occur within 24 hours of the time the temperature drops below 99 degrees F.

Never leave your bitch to whelp unattended, as Shih Tzu frequently whelp their puppies rear feet first and often do not cut umbilical cords or clean off the puppies themselves. You *must* be there to assist. In addition, this is a small bitch having large-headed puppies who may well need aid, even though Caesarean sections in our breed aren't very common. Also, never assume that a bred bitch didn't take unless you've had her x-rayed. Sometimes a good-sized bitch with only one puppy gives no sign of being pregnant until she delivers.

WHELPING THE LITTER

The start of hard labor is unmistakable. The bitch will contract vigorously, often standing up and grunting during a contraction and panting heavily afterward. Watch her vulva carefully. When you see what looks like a translucent, water-filled balloon, a puppy will soon emerge. The rectal-vulva area will swell as the puppy reaches it, and the bitch may cry out or snap at her rear. If part of the puppy is visible and the bitch seems unable to push it out with a few further hard contractions, or if the fluid-filled sac bursts, you will have to help. Gently grasp the puppy with a towel and pull it in a downward curve in line with the vulva during each contraction. *Do not pull in between contractions,* as this can cause the bitch to hemorrhage.

Once the puppy has emerged, with or without your help, it will probably be enclosed in what looks like a plastic envelope. Quickly but calmly, tear this membrane away from the puppy's face and gently clear its nostrils and mouth with a towel. If this does not make it gasp and begin breathing, rub the puppy vigorously but gently with a towel. If this is not successful and the puppy is turning blue, use any means you can to shock it into taking a breath. Hold it between the palms of your hands, head toward your fingertips, and swing it downward from over your head to between your knees several times to clear its nasal passages. Place it alternately under hot and cold running water. Breathe gently into its nostrils and mouth. In some cases, it can take as long as a half hour to get a puppy breathing, so don't give up too quickly.

Quite often the afterbirth, which looks something like a piece of shriveled liver, will not emerge with the puppy, and the puppy

This whelping box has a "pig rail" to keep the mother from accidentally crushing her babies and plenty of soft towels so she can dig a nest as she prepares to whelp.

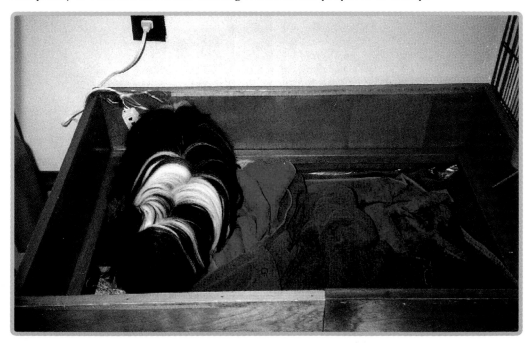

A puppy, still enclosed in its water-filled sac, is emerging. Once it is out of the birth canal, break the sac, clean the face, and get the puppy to take its first breath.

will still be attached to its mother. As long as the puppy is breathing, and you are supporting it in your hand if the mother is standing so that there is not undue tension on the umbilical cord, there is no need to rush. Usually, the afterbirth will be expelled a few contractions later. If not, once you have enough cord exposed, clamp the cord about two inches away from the puppy. Wait a few moments for the blood flow to subside, and then cut the cord on the puppy's side of the clamp (to avoid losing your hold on the placenta), preferably at the place where it seems to separate naturally. If there is bleeding, tie the cord with dental floss or press styptic powder onto the end. Do not pull on the cord if you can avoid it, and if you must, try to do so during a contraction while supporting the puppy. Otherwise you may cause the cord to break and lose the afterbirth, or create an umbilical hernia. Dispose of placentas promptly; do not allow the mother to eat them, as they are likely to give her diarrhea.

Once a puppy is dry and breathing, encourage it to nurse by squeezing a drop of milk out of one of the bitch's teats and rubbing the puppy's mouth and nose over it. Some puppies begin nursing on their own while still attached to their dam by the umbilical cord, but others take more time. Rubbing a reluctant puppy with a towel often encourages it to nurse, and nursing seems to stimulate the bitch to further contractions.

Quite often, the first two puppies arrive in quick succession. It is very common, however, for a bitch to rest for an hour or so after delivering one or two puppies before having any more. If she seems calm and is busy caring for the first arrivals, just wait for her to begin contracting again. A bit of honey from a spoon will often encourage a tired bitch to begin contracting again. Some breeders give cold milk or vanilla ice cream during labor; the extra calcium can really help. Once she begins having hard contractions, move the delivered puppies out of the way onto a heating pad (set on "low" and covered with a cloth or towel) while the bitch is delivering another puppy, so that she does not accidentally step on them.

WHEN YOU NEED THE VET

It is a good idea to alert your veterinarian when labor is imminent to be sure you can reach him (or a designated alternative) quickly in case of an emergency. Keep a telephone in easy reach while whelping; you may not be able to leave the room to call the vet during an emergency. Have a clean enclosed crate close at hand with toweling inside it in case you need it for a quick journey—and a helper to warm up the car first if the weather is cold. If the bitch has been having hard contractions for two hours with no signs of a puppy, she may have a malpositioned or very large puppy and require a Caesarean section and should be taken to the vet. If the bitch's uterine muscles become too tired to contract even though she obviously still has more puppies, or if she does not expel one afterbirth for each puppy (the reason for the surgical clamp), she will

It is very important that puppies nurse during the first 72 hours, so that they will receive maternal antibodies from their mother's milk to protect them from disease.

need to go to the vet for an injection of pituitrin to restart the contractions or expel the placentas. An afterbirth problem can wait until the morning after the delivery, however, rather than upsetting the mother and her newborns. The most urgent emergency is eclampsia (a sudden drop in the calcium level in the blood), which luckily is uncommon in our breed. A bitch with eclampsia suddenly falls down and becomes rigid, spikes a very high temperature, and requires immediate veterinary attention if she is to survive.

Be sure to take someone with you to the vet and be prepared for any eventuality during your journey. I once had a bitch deliver two puppies en route in a taxicab and a third in the lobby of the apartment house where I then lived before I could get back upstairs!

AFTER THE BIRTH

Once labor is completed, and a careful palpation of the mother indicates that no puppies remain, check the puppies carefully to be sure they do not have any abnormalities. As cleft palates are a problem in any short-faced breed, examine the roof of the mouth carefully to see that it is intact. Puppies with cleft palates cannot nurse, and it is best to put them down immediately before their crying upsets the mother. (Discuss the methods for doing this with your veterinarian *before* the puppies are born.) Some newborn Shih Tzu have open fontanelles (incomplete closure of the top of the skull) at birth and sometimes for a few weeks thereafter. These "soft spots" generally close before the puppy is ready to go to its new home. You must be very careful not to hit the open area with any hard object, as you possibly could kill the puppy.

Pink noses and footpads are the norm in newborn Shih Tzu. If you want to have your veterinarian remove any dewclaws, it is best to have this done soon after birth while the toes are small. Most Shih Tzu puppies look black or black and white at birth because of the black coat tippings. You have to wait until the coat is dry and examine the hair close to the skin to determine what color the puppy will be. This is, some breeders believe, the best age to determine length of back prior to maturity, so check to see which puppies have the shortest backs. Head shape can be distorted by the trauma of birth. Also carefully weigh each puppy on a baby scale. Continue to do this every day, because a failure to gain weight is often the first indicator that a puppy is failing to thrive and needs special attention if it is to survive.

Once all of the puppies have had a good meal and gone to sleep, you can wash and dry the rear of the mother. She should have a drink of water and a light meal and be given a chance to eliminate. While a pink or greenish black discharge for a few days after whelping is common, watch carefully for signs of uterine infection (pyometritis), including a foul-smelling discharge, extreme thirst, vomiting and dehydration, bloodshot eyes, or an elevated temperature. Pyometritis is a true medical emergency that, if not treated promptly, could cost you both your bitch and your puppies.

After whelping, the soiled bedding in the puppy area should be replaced. Some breeders use shredded unprinted newsprint for bedding, but I prefer a bathmat or a piece of washable, low-napped carpeting taped securely with duct tape to the underside of a

With all of the puppies born and fed, clean up the mother and nest. Remove all loose and soiled bedding from the whelping box so the puppies will not smother.

heavy piece of cardboard cut to fit the puppy enclosure. The puppy area should also contain a waterproof heating pad with a cloth cover set on low to prevent chilling; allow enough room for the puppies to crawl off the heating pad if it becomes uncomfortably warm and cover the electrical wires so that they cannot be chewed by either the mother or the puppies. As the mother often nests vigorously for several days after whelping, a puppy could easily be smothered in loose heavy bedding such as bath towels. Indoor-outdoor carpeting is not suitable for use in puppy enclosures, as urine releases a chemical that can burn tender puppy skin.

Once you have returned the mother to her babies in their clean, dry, and warm nest, and the puppies are all nursing contentedly under her proud eyes, you can relax a bit. You can also give yourself a pat on the back if all has gone well, even though a bit earlier it may have seemed as if you were all thumbs and needed at least four pairs of hands. Rest assured, it does get easier with practice!

It is very important that puppies nurse from their mother, if at all possible, during at least the first 72 hours after birth. Placing your fingers on each side of a reluctant puppy's mouth helps to form a good suction. Rubbing a puppy that is slow to nurse may stimulate it enough to get it going. If, however, you have a puppy (or several puppies) that are failing to thrive, or if the dam has insufficient milk, be sure you have learned beforehand from an experienced breeder how to bottle-feed or tube-feed tiny Shih Tzu puppies. This is a critical skill if you are to save your babies. Tube-feed only puppies less than one week old, as there is less chance of pneumonia with bottle-feeding. Watch carefully to see that all of the puppies are getting enough to eat. Puppies that are not gaining weight, are listless and limp, or fail to nurse eagerly may need supplementary feeding.

An orphan puppy will need to receive about 1 cc per ounce of body weight every two hours during the first week and every four hours during the second week. (The amount of time between feedings can be increased as the puppy grows.) Use premixed liquid puppy formula, heated gently on the stove in a pan of warm water until it is warm, but *not* hot; do not heat the formula in the microwave, as this breaks down its nutrients. Do not allow the milk to flow too freely if you are bottle feeding, as the puppy can inhale the fluid and choke on it or come down with pneumonia from fluid in the lungs. Be sure not to overfeed—the puppy should be pear-shaped, rather than having a tightly

Once your healthy puppies are up on their feet, they can be introduced to the latter food in the same way. They should be fed small quantities four or five times a day and be weaned by the sixth week. Do not leave stale food sitting in the nest. Feed only what the puppies will consume rapidly and increase the quantity as they grow. Their mother will clean up the nest until you begin to introduce puppy food, at which time this delightful job will become yours!

A newborn Shih Tzu puppy often has a pink nose and footpads. This puppy's umbilical cord has been tied with unwaxed dental floss. It will fall off in a few days.

distended tummy. At the first sign of pneumonia, visit your vet so that he can administer the appropriate antibiotics. Diarrhea also requires an immediate trip to the vet, as this can kill a tiny puppy quickly. A drop of honey may help strengthen a very weak puppy so that it will be able to nurse. By the third week, encourage the puppy to lick a bit of a mixture of rice baby cereal and jarred meat baby food off your finger. By four weeks, you can add well-soaked puppy kibble to this mixture.

While your dam is nursing, she should receive extra food and water to help her produce milk; feeding her puppy food at this time provides her with increased calcium. Watch, however, to be sure that her breasts are being emptied at each feeding. Excess milk can lead to red and tender breasts and, ultimately, to mastitis. Hot compresses, a temporary reduction in food and water, and the gentle expression of excess milk can help to ward off such an infection, which might mean having to remove the mother from the puppies altogether.

At one week of age your puppy still cannot see or hear. Nevertheless, you should begin to accustom it to human contact by picking it up and stroking it gently. (Carlene Snyder)

SOCIALIZING SHIH TZU BABIES

Young Shih Tzu puppies need constant love and attention as they grow. There have been many good books and articles written on the subject of socializing young puppies. Take the time to read a few before you have a litter so that you will be a knowledgeable breeder and your puppies will make good companions. Also read about puppy temperament testing, so that you will be able to make an intelligent match between buyer and puppy.

Research has shown that certain periods in a young puppy's life are critical in developing a happy, healthy adult. During the first two weeks after birth, handle the puppies gently each day, stroking them and turning them around in your hands. Keep the whelping area generally quiet to avoid upsetting the mother, although the puppies can see very little for several days after their eyes open and are born unable to hear. During the third week, continue this gentle handling and stress-free environment. Because the puppies can now hear, you should also talk to them in a pleasant tone of voice. They will begin to notice their littermates during this time, and to learn appropriate canine behavior from their mother.

Real learning begins during the fourth week, when your puppies play with each other and their mother and learn more about canine behavior. By this age, you can take each puppy away from its mother and littermates for 10–15 minutes twice a day and snuggle it and play with it gently. Encourage the puppy to explore different parts of your home but be sure it does not become stressed.

For the first few weeks, the dam will generally provide all nourishment and clean up after her puppies. They should be weighed daily to be sure they are growing. (Kristen Schoenfeld)

At this age, the puppies can also be introduced to new sounds, such as a radio or television with the sound set at a moderate level, the doorbell, and the dishwasher, clothes dryer, and vacuum cleaner. You can put each puppy into your car so that they become familiar with it, but do not yet take them for a drive. You can also put a soft collar around the puppy's neck while you can observe him, but do not leave him unattended with the collar on, or he may injure himself severely. Continue to handle the puppies gently and avoid loud noises. Visitors should not be permitted to handle the puppies until they have received their inoculations to avoid unwittingly exposing your youngsters to disease.

As soon as your puppies begin to eat solid food, fresh water should be available to them at all times. Puppies quickly learn to drink from a guinea-pig or rabbit water bottle, which avoids messy playing in the water dish and helps strengthen the muscles that enable them to hold their heads up. Once they are up on their feet, your puppies should have a place to eliminate removed from the area where they eat and sleep; the towel or carpet-covered eating and sleeping area should be relatively small. This is the first step toward paper training, as Shih Tzu

By six weeks of age, when they have had their first shots, begin to introduce your Shih Tzu puppies to new people and new environments.

puppies are generally very clean and reluctant to eliminate where they eat and sleep. The elimination area will stay cleaner if you put a floor grate from an exercise pen or crate over the paper and/or use unprinted newsprint for the top layer. The grate will also keep the puppies from playing with and shredding the paper. Pick up all solid waste promptly to discourage stool-eating.

By three weeks of age, Shih Tzu puppies are beginning to try to sit up and walk. They can now see and hear and interact with each other.

At four-and-a-half weeks of age, your puppies will be walking and steady enough on their feet to introduce them to solid food. At first, the food's texture should be gruellike. (Kristen Schoenfeld)

During the fifth and sixth weeks, while the puppies are being weaned, they still need to spend time with their mother and littermates. At this stage they learn what is acceptable and unacceptable to other dogs. If they have spent most of their time in a quiet part of the house, they should be moved to a more public area, such as the kitchen, which should be carefully puppy-proofed so that they will not injure themselves. Let the puppies crawl over you and provide them with squeaky and tug-of-war toys and Gumabones® to ease the pain of teething. One favorite puppy game, often called "king of the roost," uses a box that puppies can climb up on and survey the world. They will contest each other to hold the coveted position on top of the box. A good Shih Tzu mother will encourage a shy puppy to become more aggressive and will discipline a very aggressive one.

While you can introduce puppies to children at this age, especially children over the age of six, be extremely careful to do so only under careful supervision—it is very easy for a young child to do serious injury to a tiny puppy with only normal handling. Always make children sit on the floor to hold a puppy, to make sure they do not drop it and injure it.

Continue early housebreaking, being sure to praise a puppy profusely when it eliminates outside or on the paper. Shih Tzu generally respond much better to praise than to correction, and you will find that suddenly a light will dawn, and the puppy will begin to eliminate in the proper place regularly. Continue the praise, and clean up indoor accidents to prevent an odor that will induce the puppy to repeat its mistake. Do not allow young puppies on your carpets or furniture unless they have recently eliminated. The

Eight to ten weeks is a good age to introduce Shih Tzu puppies to children, being sure both are carefully supervised. (Ann Bromley and Sally Watkeys)

Many buyers request a puppy for Christmas. This is *not* a good time to introduce a new puppy to the household. It is best to put a photo and some supplies under the tree and schedule the puppy's arrival after the holiday confusion is over, so that it does not get overlooked or overwhelmed. (Florence V. Duffield)

fewer opportunities there are for them to make mistakes, the fewer bad habits they will develop, and the easier it will be for their new owners to complete their training.

As all of their experiences to this point should have been pleasant ones, your puppies should be happy with their world and with people. Once they have had their first shots, take each of them out individually several times a week to shopping centers, parks, and other places. Allow people to pet and talk to each puppy while you are holding it, praising it, and reassuring it. This is also the time to begin individually crate training your puppies and taking them out of doors after meals to initiate outdoors housebreaking as well as get them accustomed to another environment. You can encourage your puppies to learn to come by backing away from them while clapping your hands and calling them to you. When they come, praise them profusely.

This is the stage at which your puppies should become accustomed to lying on their backs in your lap to be brushed and having their nails and footpads trimmed (necessary for good footing as they learn to walk) and their ears cleaned. Make grooming fun rather than a contest of wills, and be sure to include baths and sessions under the blow dryer. Avoid getting water in the puppy's nose or ears and be sure the water and dryer temperatures are comfortable. Show puppies can be accustomed to stacking on a table and having their mouths examined and their legs handled at this time also. All of the puppies should begin to respond to individual names and learn the meaning of the word "no."

Ideally, all of this training and socialization should continue, coupled with leash training, until the puppies are 12 weeks old and ready to leave for their new homes. Research has shown that the period from eight to ten weeks is the critical canine fear-imprint period. Unless the puppy's new owner is very knowledgeable and able to provide the secure and safe environment and affection the puppy needs during this critical stage, it is best to avoid undue stress that could lead to chronic adult behavior problems. Immunizations should be scheduled, if possible, before and after this stage, and the puppy should never be shipped by air until it is at least 12 weeks old (most breeders wait until 16 weeks). Also avoid harsh punishment—it is best simply to distract your puppy from a forbidden object. By this time, the puppies should be separated most of the time, to avoid having the more dominant ones subjugate the submissive ones. You should become the leader in your puppy's world, and he should be anxious to please you. Keep any training sessions short. If your puppy becomes fearful, as often happens during this stage, do not force him. Continue to speak to him cheerfully, as if nothing bad has happened. If you cuddle a puppy every time he becomes afraid, you are reinforcing fearful behavior. It is best to try to avoid fear-inducing incidents until the puppy is mature and self-confident enough to handle them. Some breeders have their puppies altered before they leave for their new homes. If you can find a vet with experience in doing this, the surgery is actually much less complex when performed at a young age. Surgical time is greatly reduced and recovery is much more rapid.

Every puppy is different, even linebred littermates. By the time you have spent many hours socializing your litter, you will have a good idea of each puppy's temperament and of which one will best suit which prospective buyer (by now you have learned as much as you can about the latter). Be proud that you have given your babies the best possible preparation for the rest of their lives—and be sure to do the same for their new owners. Hopefully, with all of this knowledge, every one of your babies will be a lovely specimen of the breed who will live a long, happy, and well-cared-for life.

By 12 weeks of age, when your puppies are old enough to leave for their new homes, they should be used to being groomed and have begun lead training. (Connie Warnock)

Recommended Reading

BOOKS ABOUT THE SHIH TZU

American Shih Tzu Club, Inc. *Historical Record Book* (multivolume).

Brearley, Joan McDonald. *The Book of the Shih Tzu.* Neptune, NJ: T.F.H. Publications, Inc., 1980.

Dadds, Audrey. *The Shih Tzu,* rev. ed. Waterlooville, England: Kingdom Books, 1995.

Easton, Allan, and Brearley, Joan McDonald. *This Is the Shih Tzu.* Neptune, NJ: T.F.H. Publications, Inc., 1980.

Ferrante, Jon, *The Shih Tzu Heritage.* Fairfax, VA: William Denlinger Publishing Co., 1989.

Joris, Victor. *The Complete Shih Tzu.* New York, NY: Howell Book House, 1994.

Mann, Clarence E., with Jayne D. Mann. *Bring on the Clowns: An Assessment of the Origin of the Shih Tzu.* New York, NY: Vantage Press, Inc., 1995.

Mitchell, Elsie P. *The Lion-Dog of Buddhist Asia.* New York, NY: Fugaisha, 1991.

Regelman, JoAnn. *A New Owner's Guide to Shih Tzu.* Neptune, NJ: T.F.H. Publications, Inc., 1996.

Seranne, Anne, with Lise M. Miller. *The Joy of Owning a Shih Tzu.* New York, NY: Howell Book House, 1982.

White, Jo Ann. *The Shih Tzu: An Owner's Guide to a Happy, Healthy Pet.* New York, NY: Howell Book House, 1995.

GENERAL USEFUL TITLES

Ackerman, DVM, Lowell. *Owner's Guide to Dog Health,* Neptune, NJ: TFH Publications, Inc., 1996.

——. *Skin and Coat Care for Your Dog,* Neptune, NJ: TFH Publications, Inc., 1996.

American Kennel Club. *The Complete Dog Book.* New York, NY: Howell Book House, 1998.

——. *American Kennel Club Dog Care and Training.* New York, NY: Howell Book House, 1991.

Battaglia, Dr. Carmen. *Breeding Better Dogs.* Neptune, NJ: T.F.H. Publications, Inc., 1986.

Benjamin, Carol Lea. *Second Hand Dog.* New York, NY: Howell Book House, 1988.

Carlson, Delbert G., and James M. Giffin. *Dog Owner's Home Veterinary Handbook.* New York, NY: Howell Book House, 1992.

Cecil, Barbara, and Gerianne and Darnell. *Competitive Obedience for the Small Dog.* Council Bluffs, IA: T9E Publishing, 1994.

Davis, Kathy Diamond. *Therapy Dogs: Training Your Dog to Reach Others.* New York, NY: Howell Book House, 1992.

De Prisco, Andrew and James B. Johnson, *The Most Complete Dog Book Ever Published: Canine Lexicon.* Neptune, NJ: TFH Publications, Inc. 1990.

Elliott, Rachel Paige. *The New Dogsteps,* 2d ed. New York, NY: Howell Book House, 1988.

Forsyth, Jane and Robert. *Forsyth Guide to Successful Dog Showing.* New York, NY: Howell Book House, 1975.

Hogg, Peggy A., and Dr. Robert J. Berndt. *Grooming and Showing Toy Dogs.* Fairfax, VA.: William Denlinger Publishing Co., 1976.

Kalstone, Shirlee. *How to Housebreak Your Dog in Seven Days.* New York: Bantam, 1985.

Martin, Eva M. *Agility Training for the Small Dog, #1: An Overview* (book-and-video package). San Marino, Calif.: Agility Productions, 1995.

Pryor, Karen. *Don't Shoot the Dog! The New Art of Teaching and Training.* New York: Bantam, 1985.

Walkowicz, Christine and Bonnie Wilcox, DVM *The Atlas of Dog Breeds of the World.* Neptune, NJ: TFH Publications, Inc., 1989.

Willis, Malcolm B. *Genetics of the Dog.* New York, NY: Howell Book House, 1989.

PERIODICALS, PAMPHLETS, AND VIDEOS

American Shih Tzu Club, Inc. *1995 Breeder Education Symposium: The Shih Tzu Standard* (video).

——. *American Shih Tzu Club Bulletin* (periodical). Editor, 4593 Old Stilesboro Rd., Acworth, GA 30101.

——. *Shih Tzu in Obedience* (video).

——. *Shih Tzu Around the World* (video).

——. *The Shih Tzu in Agility* (video).

——. *Your Shih Tzu: Care and Training* (booklet).

Cecil, Barbara, and Gerianne Darnell, *Competitive Obedience Training for the Small Dog: Canine Training Systems—Small dog Fun* (3 videos). Council Bluffs, IA: T9E Publishing, 1996.

Comprehensive Shih Tzu Grooming. (video). Twin Cities Area Shih Tzu Club, 3352 Beard Ave. N., Robbinsdale, MN 55422.

Pryor, Karen. *Clicker Magic* (video).

The Shih Tzu (video). The American Kennel Club, Inc.

The Shih Tzu Reporter (periodical). Reporter Publications, P.O. Box 6369, Los Osos, CA 93412.

SOME INTERESTING WEB SITES FOR THE COMPUTER-LITERATE

ASTC Web Site: http://www.akc.org/clubs/astc/index.html or http://www.shihtzu.org
Dog Shows and Related Information: http//www.infodog.com
T.F.H. Publications: http://www.tfh.com
Travel with Your Dog: http//www.traveldog.com
Veterinary Medicine Web Sites:
http://www.uncc.edu/lis/library/reference/human/k9vetmed.htm
http://www.teleport.com/~gback/cghp.html
http://www.netrover.com/~eyevet/info.html (veterinary opthamology)
http://www2.computerland.net/ofa/index2.htm (Orthopedic Foundation for Animals)
http://www.ahdl.msu.edu/ahdl/endo.htm (thyroid problems)

Index

Page numbers in **boldface** refer to illustrations. Entries do not refer to *The Illustrated Guide to the Shih Tzu Standard*, which follows this index and is paginated separately.

Index

Illustrated Guide
to the
Shih Tzu Standard

American Shih Tzu Club, Inc.

Preface

This publication was produced by the American Shih Tzu Club, Inc. The computer imaging was provided by the American Kennel Club, Inc. Judging Research and Development Department. This guide is published by special arrangement with T.F.H Publications, Inc. for the sole purpose of creating a better understanding and knowledge of the breed standard for the Shih Tzu. It is intended for use by breeders, exhibitors, judges, and novices to gain a greater insight into and appreciation of our breed.

Thank you to primary artist Stephen Hubbell for his excellent illustrations. Artists Pam Powers and Cora Lee Romano also contributed to the sketches.

Credit goes to Alex Smith Photography for their patience with the before-and-after photographs and to all members who submitted photographs and ideas. Photo credits to Allan Brown, Terry Carter, Alan Ellsworth, Greg & Tammi Larsen, Joan & Tom McGee, Betty Medlinger, Pets by Paulette, Wendy & Richard Paquette, Haruyoshi Ueda, and Missy Yuhl. Last but not least our appreciation to Richard Paquette for assistance in the design of this guide.

Illustrated Guide to the Shih Tzu Standard
© 1997, American Shih Tzu Club, Inc.

Committee

Wendy Paquette , Chairperson
Peter J. Rogers III
Joe Walton

Computer Imaging © 1995, American Kennel Club, Inc.
Published by special arrangement with T.F.H. Publications, Inc.

Contents

History of the Breed

The legend of the Shih Tzu has come to us from documents, paintings, and objects d'art dating from A.D. 624. During the Tang Dynasty, K'iu T'ai, King of Viqur, gave the Chinese court a pair of dogs, said to have come from the Fu Lin (assumed to be the Byzantine Empire). Mention of these dogs was again made in A.D. 990-994 when people of the Ho Chou sent dogs as tribute.

Another theory of their introduction to China was recorded in the mid-seventeenth century when dogs were brought from Tibet to the Chinese court. These dogs were bred in the Forbidden City of Beijing. Many pictures of them were kept in *The Imperial Dog Book*. The smallest of these dogs resembled a lion, as represented in Oriental art. In Buddhist belief, there is an association between the lion and their deity. Shih Tzu means lion. The dogs for court breeding were selected with great care. From these the Shih Tzu known today developed. They were often called "the chrysanthemum-faced dog" because the hair grows about the face in all directions.

These dogs were small, intelligent, and extremely docile. It is known that the breeding of the Shih Tzu was delegated to certain court eunuchs who vied with each other to produce specimens that would take the Emperor's fancy. Those that were selected had their pictures painted on hangings or tapestries, and the eunuchs who were responsible for the dogs were given gifts by the Emperor.

It is known that the Shih Tzu was a house pet during most of the Qing (Manchu) Dynasty and that the breed was highly favored by the royal family. At the time of the Communist Revolution, a large number of dogs were destroyed and the breed became extinct in China.

Around 1930, Lady Brownrigg, an Englishwoman living in China, was fortunate to find a few of these dogs, which she imported to England. These, with a few salvaged by diplomats stationed in China, made up the stock which was responsible for the continuation of the breed in Europe.

From England and Scandinavia Shih Tzu were sent to other countries in Europe and to Australia. During World War II, members of the Armed Forces stationed in England became acquainted with the breed and on their return brought some back to the United States, thus introducing them to this country.

The Shih Tzu was admitted to registration in the American Kennel Club Stud Book in March 1969 and to regular show classification in the Toy Group at AKC shows September 1, 1969.

Anatomy

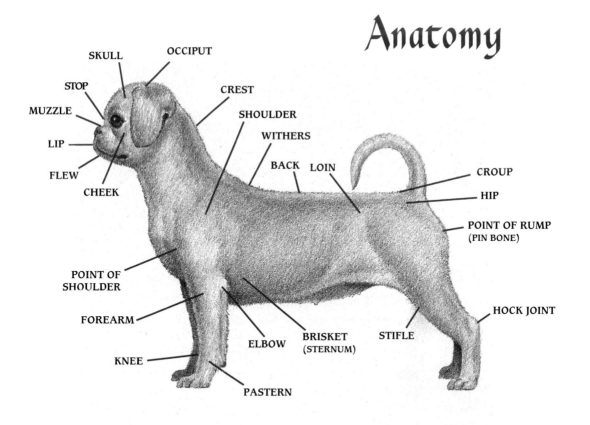

SKULL
OCCIPUT
STOP
CREST
MUZZLE
SHOULDER
LIP
WITHERS
FLEW
BACK
LOIN
CHEEK
CROUP
HIP
POINT OF RUMP
(PIN BONE)
POINT OF
SHOULDER
HOCK JOINT
FOREARM
ELBOW
BRISKET
(STERNUM)
STIFLE
KNEE
PASTERN

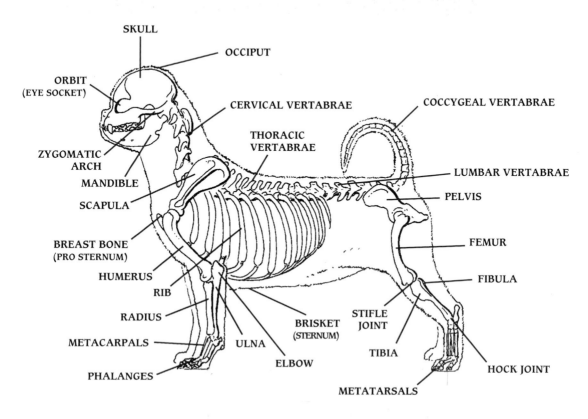

SKULL
OCCIPUT
ORBIT
(EYE SOCKET)
CERVICAL VERTABRAE
COCCYGEAL VERTABRAE
THORACIC
VERTABRAE
ZYGOMATIC
ARCH
LUMBAR VERTABRAE
MANDIBLE
PELVIS
SCAPULA
BREAST BONE
(PRO STERNUM)
FEMUR
HUMERUS
FIBULA
RIB
RADIUS
STIFLE
JOINT
METACARPALS
ULNA
TIBIA
HOCK JOINT
ELBOW
BRISKET
(STERNUM)
PHALANGES
METATARSALS

Standard for the Shih Tzu

Approved May 9, 1989

GENERAL APPEARANCE

The Shih Tzu is a sturdy, lively, alert Toy dog with long flowing double coat. Befitting his noble Chinese ancestry as a highly valued, prized companion and palace pet, the Shih Tzu is proud of bearing, has a distinctively arrogant carriage with head well up and tail curved over the back. Although there has always been considerable size variation, the Shih Tzu must be compact, solid, carrying good weight and substance.

Even though a Toy dog, the Shih Tzu must be subject to the same requirements of soundness and structure prescribed for all breeds, and any deviation from the ideal described in the standard should be penalized to the extent of the deviation. Structural faults common to all breeds are as undesirable in the Shih Tzu as in any other breed, regardless of whether or not such faults are specifically mentioned in the standard.

SIZE, PROPORTION, SUBSTANCE

Size—Ideally, height at withers is 9 to 10 1/2 inches; but, not less than 8 inches nor more than 11 inches. Ideally, weight of mature dogs, 9 to 16 pounds

Proportion—Length between withers and root of tail is slightly longer than height at withers. *The Shih Tzu must never be so high stationed as to appear leggy, nor so low stationed as to appear dumpy or squatty.*

Substance—Regardless of size, the Shih Tzu is always compact, solid and carries good weight and substance.

HEAD

Head—Round, broad, wide between eyes, its size *in balance* with the overall size of dog being neither too large nor too small.

Fault: Narrow head, close-set eyes.

Expression—Warm, sweet, wide-eyed, friendly and trusting. An overall well-balanced and pleasant expression supercedes the importance of individual parts. *Care should be taken to look and examine well beyond the hair to determine if what is seen is the actual head and expression rather than an image created by grooming technique.*

Eyes—Large, round, not prominent, placed well apart, looking straight ahead. *Very dark.* Lighter on liver pigmented dogs and blue pigmented dogs.

Fault: Small, close-set or light eyes; excessive eye white.

Ears—Large, set slightly below crown of skull; heavily coated.

Skull—Domed.

Stop—*There is a definite stop.*

Muzzle—Square, short, unwrinkled, with good cushioning, set no lower than bottom eye rim; never downturned. Ideally, no longer than 1 inch from tip of nose to stop, although length may vary slightly in relation to overall size of dog. Front of muzzle should be flat; lower lip and chin not protruding and definitely never receding.

Fault: Snippiness, lack of definite stop.

Nose—Nostrils are broad, wide, and open.

Pigmentation—Nose, lips, eye rims are black on all colors, except liver on liver pigmented dogs and blue on blue pigmented dogs.

Fault: Pink on nose, lips, or eye rims.

Bite—Undershot. Jaw is broad and wide. A missing tooth or slightly misaligned teeth should not be too severely penalized. Teeth and tongue should not show when mouth is closed.

Fault: Overshot bite.

NECK, TOPLINE, BODY

Of utmost importance is an overall well-balanced dog with no exaggerated features.

Neck—Well set-on flowing smoothly into shoulders; of sufficient length to permit natural high head carriage and in balance with height and length of dog.

Topline—Level.

Body—Short-coupled and sturdy with no waist or tuck-up. The Shih Tzu is slightly longer than tall.

Fault: Legginess.

Chest—Broad and deep with good spring-of-rib, however, not barrel-chested. Depth of ribcage should extend to just below elbow. Distance from elbow to withers is a little greater than from elbow to ground.

Croup—Flat.

Tail—Set on high, heavily plumed, carried in curve well over back. Too loose, too tight, too flat, or too low set a tail is undesirable and should be penalized to extent of deviation.

FOREQUARTERS

Shoulders—Well-angulated, well laid-back, well laid-in, fitting smoothly into body.

Legs—Straight, well-boned, muscular, set well-apart and under chest, with elbows set close to body.

Pasterns—Strong, perpendicular.

Dewclaws—May be removed.

Feet—Firm, well-padded, point straight ahead.

HINDQUARTERS

Angulation of hindquarters should be in balance with forequarters.

Legs—Well-boned, muscular, and straight when viewed from rear with well-bent stifles, not close set but in line with forequarters.

Hocks—Well let down, perpendicular.

Fault: Hyperextension of hocks.

Dewclaws—May be removed.

Feet—Firm, well-padded, point straight ahead.

COAT

Luxurious, double-coated, dense, long, and flowing. Slight wave permissible. Hair on top of head is tied up.

Fault: Sparse coat, single coat, curly coat.

Trimming—Feet, bottom of coat, and anus may be done for neatness and to facilitate movement.

Fault: Excessive trimming.

COLOR AND MARKINGS

All are permissible and to be considered *equally.*

GAIT

The Shih Tzu moves straight and must be shown at its own natural speed, *neither raced nor strung-up*, to evaluate its smooth, flowing, effortless movement with good front reach and equally strong rear drive, level topline, naturally high head carriage, and tail carried in a gentle curve over back.

TEMPERAMENT

As the sole purpose of the Shih Tzu is that of a companion and house pet, it is essential that its temperament be outgoing, happy, affectionate, friendly and trusting towards all.

General Appearance

The Shih Tzu is a sturdy, lively, alert Toy dog with long flowing double coat. Befitting his noble Chinese ancestry as a highly valued, prized companion and palace pet, the Shih Tzu is proud of bearing, has a distinctively arrogant carriage with head well up and tail curved over the back. Although there has always been considerable size variation, the Shih Tzu must be compact, solid, carrying good weight and substance.

Even though a Toy dog, the Shih Tzu must be subject to the same requirements of soundness and structure prescribed for all breeds, and any deviation from the ideal described in the standard should be penalized to the extent of the deviation. Structural faults common to all breeds are as undesirable in the Shih Tzu as in any other breed, regardless of whether or not such faults are specifically mentioned in the standard.

Size, Proportion, Substance

Size

Ideally, height at withers is 9 to 10 1/2 inches; but, not less than 8 inches nor more than 11 inches. Ideally, weight of mature dogs—9 to 16 pounds.

Clarification—It should be stressed that overall balance and quality should be of utmost importance, regardless of whether a particular dog falls into the lower or higher end of the ideals set forth in the standard.

It should also be noted that the proper dense and double coat may make a particular dog appear larger in size than it is in actuality.

Substance

Regardless of size, the Shih Tzu is *always* compact, solid and carries good weight and substance.

Clarification—A Shih Tzu should never be narrow or slab sided and should have a good amount of overall bone. Young or immature dogs should not be penalized for carrying less weight, providing the overall frame, bone, and muscle tone projects a dog with good substance. When picked up, the Shih Tzu should be surprisingly heavy for its size.

Proportion

Length between the withers and root of the tail is slightly longer than height at withers. *The Shih Tzu must never be so high stationed as to appear leggy, nor so low stationed as to appear dumpy or squatty.*

Clarification—The Shih Tzu should be a rectangular dog not a square dog. When judging whether a dog is of correct proportions, one must train the eye to measure the back from withers to root of tail and compare it to the height of the withers. The correct dog will be longer in back than it is tall. However, when the total length of the Shih Tzu is measured from the breast bone (prosternum) to the point of the rump (pin bone), the Shih Tzu is a rectangular dog. Proper head carriage, tail set and sufficient length of body will also give the desired look of a rectangular dog with a smooth, flowing and effortless gait resulting in the style and carriage so distinctive in ideal dogs.

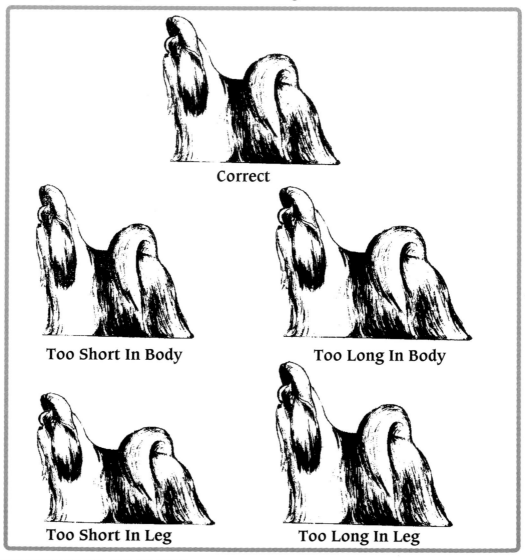

Correct

Too Short In Body

Too Long In Body

Too Short In Leg

Too Long In Leg

Proportion

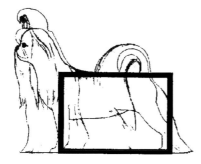

Too Short In Body

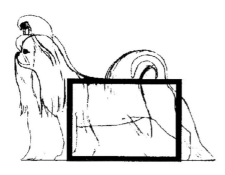

Correct

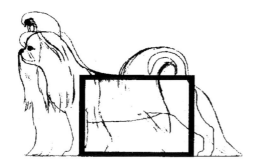
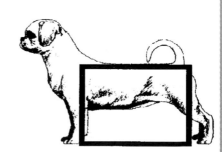

Too Long In Body

Head

Head

Round, broad, wide between eyes, its size *in balance* with the overall size of the dog being neither too large nor too small.

Fault: Narrow head, close-set eyes.

Clarification—No individual part should take prominence over another. The individual parts of the head should combine to produce a pleasing expression.

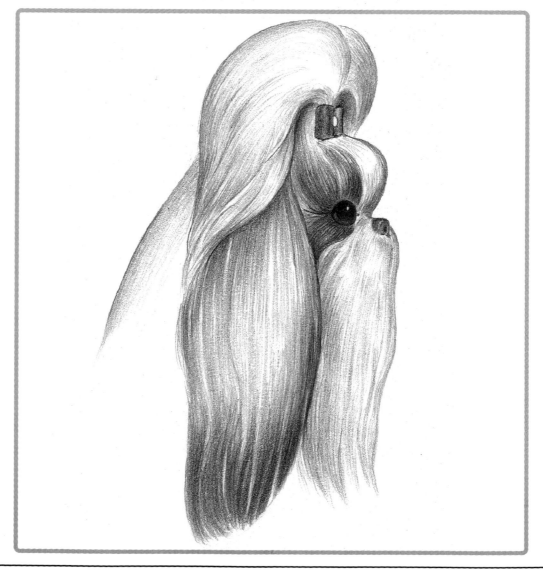

Expression

Warm, sweet, wide-eyed, friendly and trusting. An overall well-balanced and pleasant expression supercedes the importance of the individual parts. *Care should be taken to look and examine well beyond the hair to determine if what is seen is the actual head and expression rather than an image created by grooming technique.*

Clarification—The Shih Tzu should never have a hard or stern expression. As the standard specifically outlines, the head should be thoroughly examined by hand to determine the actual size, shape and expression.

Eyes

Large, round, not prominent, placed well apart, looking straight ahead. *Very dark.* Lighter on liver pigmented dogs and blue pigmented dogs.
Fault: Small, close-set or light eyes; excessive eye white.

Clarification—A dog may show some eye white, but it should never be so much that it detracts from the warm, sweet expression of the Shih Tzu.

Ears

Large, set slightly below crown of skull; heavily coated.

Clarification—Ears should blend into the head.

Skull

Domed.

Clarification—The skull should be well domed and rounded or arched in all directions. The skull should never be flat. The skull should never fall away behind the eyes. There should be a good amount of foreskull between and in front of the eyes.

Stop

There is a definite stop.

Clarification—The stop is a distinct definition between the skull and the muzzle and should be deep. There is no wrinkle such as that found on the Pug or Pekingese.

Muzzle

Square, short, unwrinkled, with good cushioning, set no lower than bottom eye rim; never downturned. Ideally, no longer than 1 inch from tip of nose to stop, although length may vary slightly in relation to overall size of dog. Front of muzzle should be flat; lower lip and chin not protruding and definitely never receding.

Fault: Snippiness, lack of definite stop.

Clarification—When viewed from the front, the muzzle should form a square, being wide from top to bottom and from side to side. The muzzle should also be viewed from the side to be sure of proper nose–eye placement. Viewed from the side, the muzzle should be perpendicular to the skull. In order to have a square muzzle, it is extremely important for the jaw to be broad or wide. A strong, broad underjaw is integral in creating the proper expression as well as the correct muzzle shape. The muzzle cushioning contributes to the desired "soft" expression.

Nose

Nostrils are broad, wide, and open.

Clarification—It should be noted that the Shih Tzu is a brachycephalic breed with a tendency for the nostrils to be pinched. Therefore it is very important that a Shih Tzu have the desired broad, wide, and open nostrils in order to have sufficient nasal capacity.

Pigmentation

Nose, lips, eye rims are black on all colors, except liver on liver pigmented dogs and blue on blue pigmented dogs

Fault: Pink on nose, lips, or eye rims.

Bite

Undershot. Jaw is broad and wide. A missing tooth or slightly misaligned teeth should not be too severely penalized. Teeth and tongue should not show when mouth is closed.
Fault: Overshot bite.

Clarification—This section of the standard should be read in conjunction with the section on muzzle. In judging whether a bite is too undershot, the muzzle should be viewed from the side as well. A bite which is too undershot, when viewed from the side, cannot be perpendicular, as required in the section on muzzle. If, when viewed from the side, the muzzle is tilted back giving a "scooped faced" appearance, the bite is too undershot, regardless of whether the teeth show. If the bite is level or overshot, the muzzle will fall away or recede.

The ideal undershot bite is one in which the outer surface of the upper teeth engages, or nearly engages, the inner surface of the lower teeth. This bite is often referred to as a "reverse scissors bite."

The reference to "missing and slightly misaligned teeth" should not be used as an excuse to encourage poorly aligned teeth. It should be remembered that the Shih Tzu has shallowly rooted teeth and may lose a tooth at a relatively young age. The width of the jaw is more important than perfect dentition.

Ideal Undershot Bite

**Correct Wide and Broad
Bite with Full Dentition**

Neck, Topline, Body

Of utmost importance is an overall well-balanced dog with no exaggerated features.

Neck

Well set on flowing smoothly into shoulders: of sufficient length to permit natural high head carriage and in balance with height and length of dog

Clarification—The neck should be in balance with the overall dog. A neck that is too long is as objectionable as a neck that is too short in that both destroy the overall balance of the Shih Tzu.

Body

Short-coupled and sturdy with no waist or tuck-up. The Shih Tzu is slightly longer than tall.
Fault: Legginess.

Clarification—Short-coupled refers to the part of the body between the last rib and the pelvis. The Shih Tzu body should be approximately the same width across from rib cage to rear, when viewed from above. There is no "waist". The body is firmly knit together and should be slightly longer than tall. The proper balanced Shih Tzu should never be leggy or too short in leg. There will be some degree of tuck-up, but this should never be to the degree found in some Hound breeds.

Chest

Broad and deep with good spring of rib, however not barrel chested. Depth of rib cage should extend to just below elbow. Distance from elbows to withers is a little greater than from elbow to ground.

Croup

Flat.

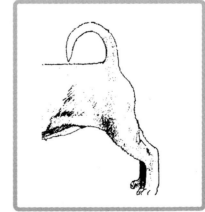

Topline

Level.

Clarification—The topline should be level, smooth and hard. Because a topline can be made to appear level when standing or stacked on a table for examination, particular attention should be paid to the topline when the dog is moving. The topline should be level when moving.

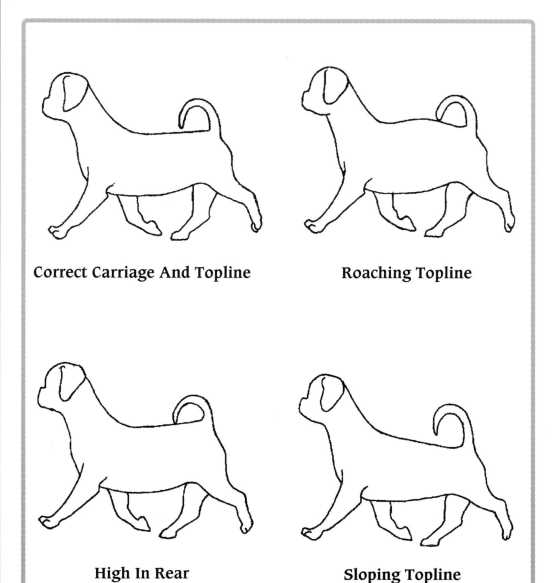

Correct Carriage And Topline

Roaching Topline

High In Rear

Sloping Topline

Tail

Set on high, heavily plumed, carried in a curve well over the back. Too loose, too tight, too flat, or too low set a tail is undesirable and should be penalized to the extent of the deviation.

Clarification—An improper tail-set and/or carriage will detract from the desired balance and outline of the Shih Tzu. The tail should be held in a gentle curve over the back. The tail should not flag or lay flat on the back.

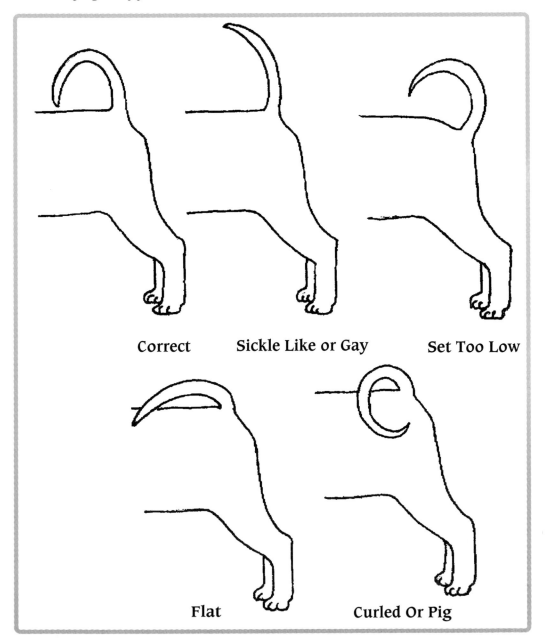

Correct   **Sickle Like or Gay**   **Set Too Low**

Flat   **Curled Or Pig**

Forequarters

Shoulders

Well angulated, well laid back, well laid in, fitting smoothly into the body.

Clarification—The shoulders should not be loaded (excessive development of muscles on the outside of the shoulder blade) or so straight that they protrude from the topline and interrupt the smooth transition from the neck, to the shoulder, to the withers.

Legs

Straight, well-boned, muscular, set well-apart and under chest, with elbows set close to body.

Clarification—The front legs should be straight from the elbow to the pasterns. The forelegs should be well-boned, muscular, and set well apart to support the broad, deep chest. The elbows should never be out or loose.

Pasterns

Strong, perpendicular.

Clarification—There must be some flex in the pastern as it contributes to the ease of the trotting gait.

Dewclaws

May be removed.

Feet

Firm, well-padded, point straight ahead.

Clarification—The feet should be well-cushioned, and thick, and the paw pads should be rough. The foot is not a part of the leg and may toe out very slightly.

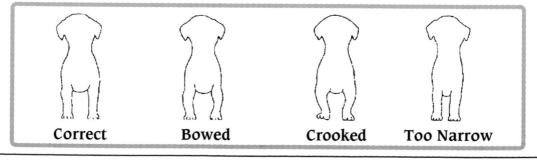

| Correct | Bowed | Crooked | Too Narrow |

Forequarters and Hindquarters

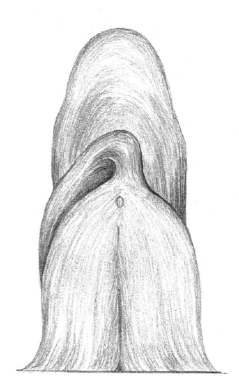

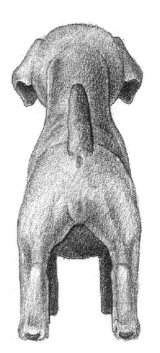

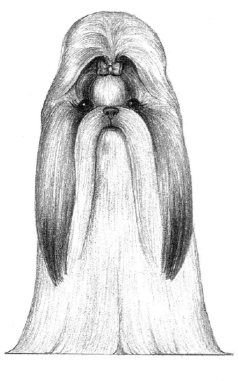

Hindquarters

Angulation of hindquarters should be in balance with the forequarters.

Legs

Well-boned, muscular, and straight when viewed from the rear with well-bent stifles, not close set but in line with the forequarters.

Clarification—The rear legs should be in proportion with the front legs in both bone and musculature. The stifles should be well-turned in order to provide the desired amount of angulation to be in balance with the forequarters.

Hocks

Well let down, perpendicular.
Fault: Hyperextension of hocks.
Clarification—The hock should not be long and should be short enough to provide sufficient leverage for the desired strong driving rear movement. The hock should be perpendicular to the ground when the dog is standing. Some Shih Tzu have luxating or double-jointed hocks as well as a tendency for the tendons that hold the joints in place to be weak, causing them to buckle forward when gentle pressure is applied to the back of the joint. This is incorrect.

Dewclaws

May be removed.

Feet

Firm, well-padded, point straight ahead.

Correct   Too Straight   Overextended

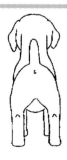 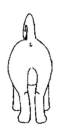 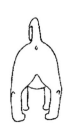 

Correct   **Cowhocked**   **Weak Joints**   **Too Narrow**

Coat

Luxurious, double-coated, dense, long, and flowing. Slight wave permissible. Hair on top of head is tied up.

Fault: Sparse coat, single coat, curly coat.

Clarification—The coat should never appear sparse or be sparse upon examination. The Shih Tzu undercoat should be soft and dense, and the outer coat should be somewhat harder and perhaps lay flatter than the undercoat. A single coat refers to a coat without the desired undercoat present. The hair on the head is generally gathered up with the use of rubber bands and a bow. The standard is not specific on how it is to be tied up, or with what. Therefore, sufficient examination of the structure of the head beneath the hair is crucial.

Trimming

Feet, bottom of coat, and anus may be done for neatness and to facilitate movement.

Fault: Excessive trimming.

Clarification—The hair between the pads on the bottom of the feet may be removed. The hair on the feet may be shaped or trimmed. The bottom of the coat may be evened or trimmed to ground length if necessary. The hair around the anus and the base of the tail may be removed.

Excessive trimming sometimes involves removing patches of hair around the neck, shoulders, and chest with clippers or scissors and should be considered excessive trimming.

Color and Markings

All are permissible and to be considered *equally*.

Clarification—All colors and markings are permissible and no color or marking should take preference over another. Dark faces or uneven markings should not be penalized and are quite acceptable.

Gait

The Shih Tzu moves straight and must be shown at its own natural speed, *neither raced or strung up*, to evaluate its smooth, flowing, effortless movement with good front reach and equally strong rear drive, level topline, naturally high head carriage, and tail carried in gentle curve over the back.

Clarification—The Shih Tzu in motion should appear as he does standing, with high head carriage and well-angulated shoulders, leading into a hard, level topline with a high tail-set. The front should move straight with the legs extending straight from the body with no toeing in or out, and the elbows should remain close to the body. From the rear, the legs should extend straight out from the body, and the pads of the feet should be visible. The Shih Tzu should never single track. The proper side movement emphasizes the balance between the front and the rear, and there should be no bounce or roll to the gait.

The wording in the standard, "strung up", does NOT mean the Shih Tzu should be shown on a "dead loose lead." The exhibitor should be able to have enough tension in the lead to guide and direct the dog, especially young not fully trained dogs. However, a dog should NOT be shown on an extremely tight lead which tends to lift the forequarters off the ground. Excessive speed in the ring makes it extremely difficult to evaluate proper movement.

Temperament

As the sole purpose of the Shih Tzu is that of a companion and house pet, it is essential that its temperament be outgoing, happy, affectionate, friendly, and trusting towards all.

Clarification—Any tendency towards shyness, snappiness, or aggressive behavior should be severely penalized. The tail should be carried proudly over the back when moving and being examined.

Essence of Shih Tzu Breed Type

Those *essential* characteristics of the Shih Tzu which distinguish it as an outstanding representative of the breed.

Temperament: Outgoing, lively, alert, proud, arrogant, affectionate, friendly and trusting.

Head: Round, broad, with eyes large, round and dark; the expression is warm, friendly and trusting; head in proportion to body.

Body: Overall balance and proportion is rectangular; well bodied, good bone, topline level, high set teacup tail.

Gait: Smooth, flowing, effortless; head and tail held high.

Coat: Long, luxurious, and double-coated.

Typical Head
Round and broad
Large dark eyes
Warm and trusting expression
Good nose placement

These photographs demonstrate the round shape of the skull when viewed from the front and the side. The eyes are large and round.

Typical Body.
Rectangular in proportion.
Good overall balance of proportion of head, size and bone.
Teacup tail.

SAME DOG AS FACING PAGE WITH HAIR REMOVED.
The overall balance of this dog is easily seen. Head is in proportion to the body. The length of neck is correct, not too long or short. The bone is balanced to the size of the dog. The legs are of good length without being too leggy or too squat. The dog is rectangular in shape with no tuck-up and an excellent teacup tail.

Note how the coated dog on the preceding page appears much taller because of the topknot; the body would also appear shorter if this dog had a full white collar/shawl.

This dog's nose and muzzle are too long and it has very little stop and foreskull. All of this is hidden by the bubble of the topknot in the coated version on the preceding page.

SAME DOG FACING FRONT.

SAME DOG WITH THE HAIR REMOVED.
Note the straight front legs, tight elbows, and broad, deep chest. The skull on this dog could be rounder and less flat with round not almond shaped eyes. Note how the coated dog on the preceding page appears much taller because of the topknot.

This example is considered extreme and not balanced. Although it is rectangular in body shape, it is too short in back. The neck is also too long.

SAME DOG AS FACING PAGE WITH HAIR REMOVED.
This dog would also be considered leggy and lacks substance. It is obvious that the hair does hide a lot of faults such as the poor topline, upright shoulder and straight rear of this dog.

This dog does have a pretty face and pleasing expression.

SAME DOG AS FACING PAGE WITH THE HAIR REMOVED.
The front legs are nice but the chest is too shallow and does not extend below the elbows.
The dog also has a high ear set.

Although this dog does not have a white blaze and symmetrical head markings, it still has a very pleasing expression.

This dog with symmetrical markings might easily give a first impression of a better head and expression, but all colors and markings are permissible.

A typical black and white.

Shih Tzu come in solid colors such as this typical black.

A typical gold and white.

A liver and white.

A gold with a black mask.

The dogs pictured above are typical eight-month-old puppies with the female on the left and a male on the right. The dogs pictured below are typical mature dogs with the female on the left and the male on the right.

A female Shih Tzu may look more feminine than her male counterpart but, as seen from these photographs, both sexes should still maintain the correct broad head with large round eyes.

Shih Tzu Movement— Smooth, flowing, effortless; head and tail held high.

The American Kennel Club, Inc.
Computer Imaging

The following pages contain computer enhanced and manipulated photographs of the Shih Tzu intended to help readers visualize various good and bad points about the breed.

To obtain the best results please look at the images and make your own conclusions about what you see. Then verify your observations by reading the clarifications and text written on the pages.

Our thanks go to Anne M. Hier of the American Kennel Club's Judging Research and Development Department, for her hard work in developing these images, and to Alex Smith Photography for providing the original photographs.

Match the coated dog to one of the lower clipped down versions.

The correct dog is dog 'b '. This dog exhibits the correct rectangular proportion, bone, substance and length of leg for the breed.

Match the coated dog to one of the lower clipped down versions.

The right match is dog '*c*' although it is not an ideal specimen of the breed. Notice how the tail and coat hide the faulty topline. This dog is also straight in shoulder and the full white collar and markings tend to give the illusion of a better front assembly. Dog '*b*' has the best shoulder layback, body and substance. Dog '*a*' lacks body and substance and is too leggy.

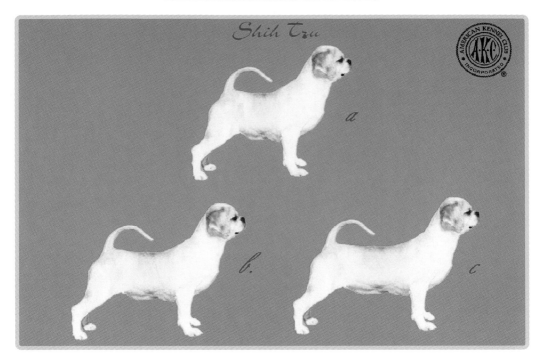

Dog '*b*' exhibits the correct proportion which overall is rectangular. All of these examples have the approximate same height while dog '*a*' is too short in body and dog '*c*' is too long in body.

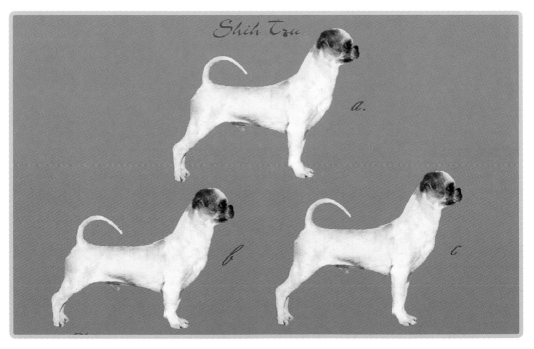

Dog '*a*' is correct. Each dog has the same length of body, while dog '*b*' is too short in leg and dog '*c*' is too leggy.

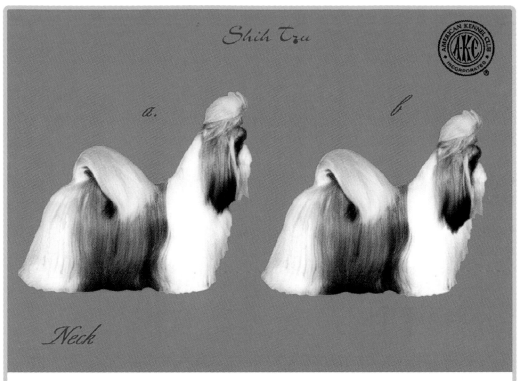

Dog '*a*' has the correct length of neck and
dog '*b*' has very little neck.

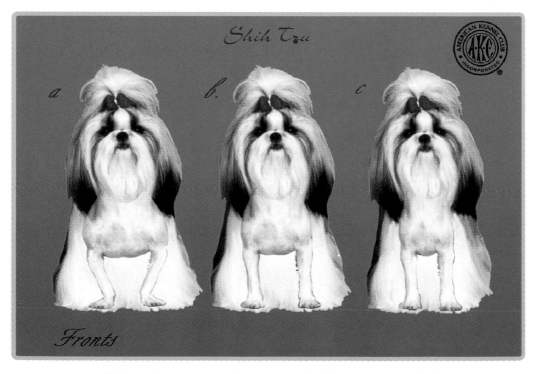

Dog '*b*' is the correct dog. Dog '*a*' has a bowed front,
and dog '*c*' is too narrow.

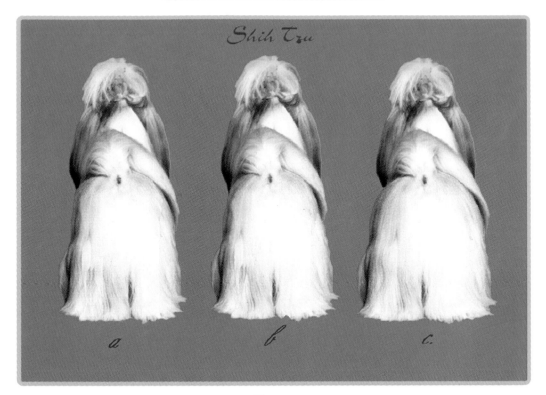

Rears

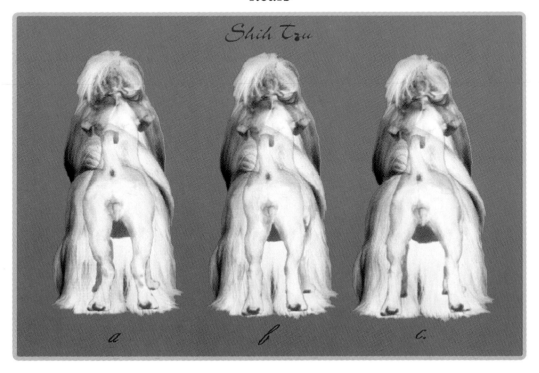

Dog '*c*' is the correct rear, dog '*a*' is cow-hocked
and dog '*b*' is too narrow.

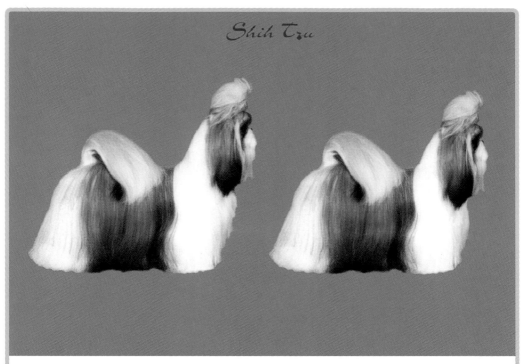

Shih Tzu

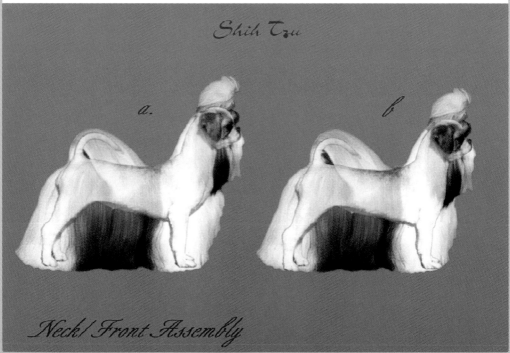

Shih Tzu

a.

b

Neck/Front Assembly

Dog '*a*' has better layback in shoulder, the correct length of neck, with the right length of leg and good forechest. Dog '*b*' is straighter in shoulder, has a short neck, is too short in leg and lacks forechest.

Dog '*b*' has the correct rear angulation,
and dog '*a*' is too straight in rear.

Dog '*b*' has the best topline but is straight in shoulder.
Dog '*a*' has a roached topline while dog '*c*' is high in the rear.

Shih Tzu

Which is the correct head?

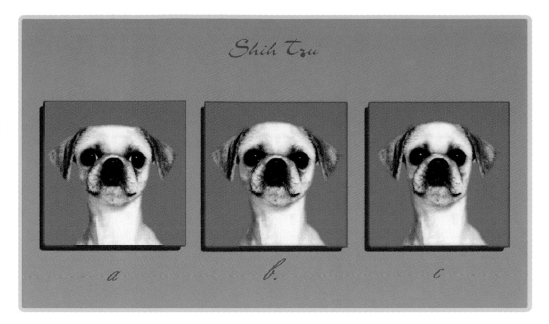

Shih Tzu

Dog '*b*' is the correct dog with a large, broad, round head with large round eyes. Dog '*a*' is too flat on top and shows white of eye. Dog '*c*' is too narrow in the skull, which results in the eyes being too close together. The ears on dog '*c*' are also set too high on the skull.

Dog '*b*' is correct. The large, round, broad skull, with large round eyes and proper nose placement add to the soft, warm, friendly expression of the Shih Tzu. Dog '*a*' is too flat on top with low set ears giving the expression a 'houndy look'. The white of eye is also not pleasing.

Dog '*b*' is correct with a large, broad and round skull. Dog '*a*' is flat on top and square looking and dog '*c*' is too domed and narrow on top.

Dog '*c*' is correct with a nice square look with a broad underjaw. Dog '*a*' has a wry look and tongue showing, and dog '*b*' is too narrow.

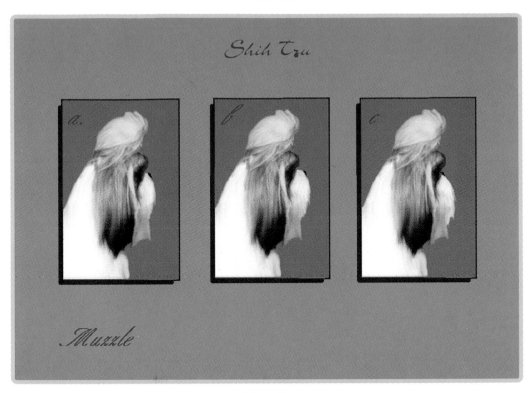

Muzzle

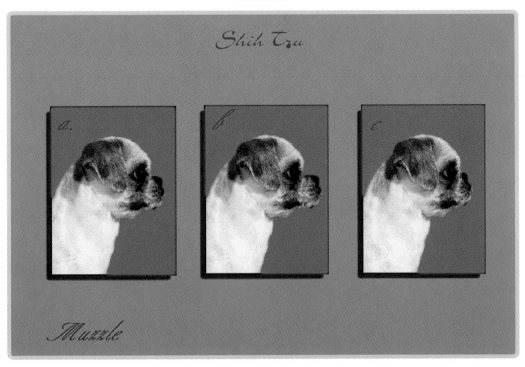

Dog '*a*' is correct with a strong, square, flat muzzle with a definite stop. Dog '*b*' is too long, and Dog '*c*' is too short and upturned.

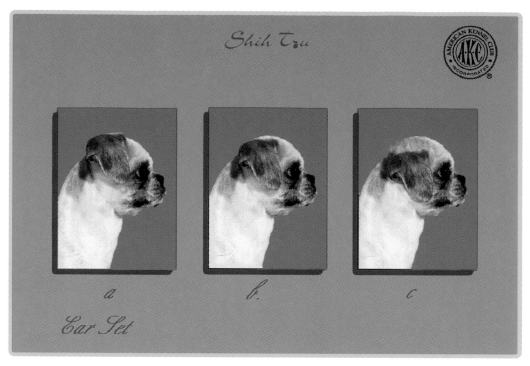

Dog '*b*' is correct with the proper ear placement.
Dog '*a*' has too high an ear set, and dog '*c*' has too low set ears.

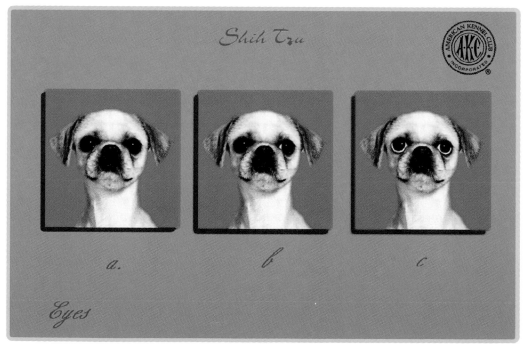

Dog '*a*' has the correct large, round and dark eye. Dog '*b*' has some
eye white showing in the corner, dog '*c*' has full eye white which is very
displeasing and gives a very scary eyed look and terrible expression.

Quiz

This quiz is based upon the Shih Tzu breed standard. It is intended to be a helpful study aid to increase your knowledge of the breed.

1. The Shih Tzu head is:
       (A) long and narrow
       (B) square and broad
       (C) large and massive
       (D) round and broad

2. The stop of the Shih Tzu is:
       (A) moderate, but distinct
       (B) very slight, but perceptible
       (C) definite stop
       (D) pronounced

3. The nose may not be:
       (A) blue on blue pigmented dogs
       (B) black
       (C) liver on liver pigmented dogs
       (D) any color

4. The following does not describe the Shih Tzu muzzle:
       (A) unwrinkled
       (B) square
       (C) tapering to the nose
       (D) never downturned

5. The following is not described as a serious fault:
       (A) narrow head, close-set eyes
       (B) snippiness
       (C) lack of definite stop
       (D) mismarked

6. The following does not describe the Shih Tzu eyes:
       (A) round and large
       (B) set well apart
       (C) prominent
       (D) looking straight ahead

7. Blue eyes:
    - (A) are a fault in all colors
    - (B) are allowed in blue pigmented dogs
    - (C) are allowed in liver dogs
    - (D) only occur in black and whites

8. The ear carriage of the Shih Tzu may be:
    - (A) long and drooping
    - (B) set level with the crown of the skull
    - (C) level with the outer corner of the eyes
    - (D) set slightly below the crown of the skull

9. The Shih Tzu bite is:
    - (A) level
    - (B) level or undershot
    - (C) scissors
    - (D) undershot

10. The expression of the Shih Tzu is:
    - (A) eager and full of interest
    - (B) soft, gentle and friendly
    - (C) warm, wide eyed, friendly and trusting
    - (D) watchful and aloof

11. The hallmark of the Shih Tzu is:
    - (A) outgoing, friendly and trusting temperament
    - (B) intelligence
    - (C) grace and agility
    - (D) long, luxurious coat

12. When judging the Shih Tzu:
    - (A) the traditional gold and white markings are preferred
    - (B) correct markings are an important consideration of type
    - (C) a white blaze and tail tip are required
    - (D) all colors and markings are to be considered equally

13. The following describes the Shih Tzu neck:
    - (A) short and thick
    - (B) in balance with height and length of dog
    - (C) slightly arched
    - (D) of good length

14. The topline of the Shih Tzu is:
               (A) level, with slight arch over the loins
               (B) sloping from withers to croup
               (C) level from withers to croup
               (D) higher at the croup than at the withers

15. The Shih Tzu tail is not:
               (A) set high
               (B) flat
               (C) heavily plumed
               (D) carried in a curve well over the back

16. In excitement, the Shih Tzu tail:
               (A) is always carried low
               (B) is curved well over the back
               (C) rises above the level of the back
               (D) may rise level with the back

17. The shoulders of the Shih Tzu are:
               (A) moderately angulated
               (B) protrude from the body
               (C) well angulated, well laid back
               (D) strongly muscled

18. The ribs of the Shih Tzu are:
               (A) barrel-chested
               (B) well-rounded
               (C) broad and deep with good spring of rib
               (D) depth should extend to just above the elbow

19. The following does not describe the Shih Tzu hindquarters:
               (A) very slightly cow hocked
               (B) well-boned
               (C) muscular
               (D) well-angulated

20. The proper Shih Tzu foot is:
               (A) oval in shape
               (B) a cat-foot
               (C) a hare-foot
               (D) firm and well padded

21. In proportion the Shih Tzu is:
    (A) compact and square
    (B) rectangular
    (C) leggy
    (D) low stationed

22. The general appearance of the Shih Tzu is a:
    (A) small dog of great power
    (B) compact, squarely proportioned dog
    (C) sturdy, lively, alert Toy dog
    (D) gay and assertive, but chary of strangers

23. Shih Tzu color should be:
    (A) symmetrical, with a full white blaze
    (B) all white
    (C) gold, with black mask favored
    (D) all colors permissible and considered equally

24. The following does not describe the Shih Tzu coat:
    (A) luxurious single coat
    (B) slight wave permissible
    (C) double-coated
    (D) dense, long and flowing

25. The Shih Tzu coat should not be:
    (A) shaped and trimmed extensively
    (B) trimmed for neatness and to facilitate movement
    (C) clean and free of tangles
    (D) luxurious and flowing

26. The Shih Tzu gait should be:
    (A) raced and strung up
    (B) short and stilted
    (C) powerful, rhythmical stride
    (D) smooth, flowing, effortless

27. The following is correct regarding Shih Tzu size:
    (A) under 8 inches at the withers is acceptable
    (B) ideally, height at the withers is 9 to 10 1/2 inches
    (C) over 11 inches at the withers is acceptable
    (D) under 8 inches or over 11 inches is a disqualification

Answers

1.   (D) round and broad
2.   (C) definite stop
3.   (D) any color
4.   (C) tapering to the nose
5.   (D) mismarked
6.   (C) prominent
7.   (A) are a fault in all colors
8.   (D) set slightly below the crown of the skull
9.   (D) undershot
10.   (C) warm, wide eyed, friendly and trusting
11.   (A) outgoing, friendly and trusting temperament
12.   (D) all colors and markings are to be considered equally
13.   (B) in balance with height and length of dog
14.   (C) level from withers to croup
15.   (B) flat
16.   (B) curved well over the back
17.   (C) well angulated, well laid back
18.   (C) broad and deep with good spring of rib
19.   (A) may be very slightly cow hocked
20.   (D) firm and well padded
21.   (B) rectangular
22.   (C) sturdy, lively, alert Toy dog
23.   (D) all colors permissible and considered equally
24.   (A) luxurious single coat
25.   (A) shaped and trimmed extensively
26.   (D) smooth, flowing, effortless
27.   (B) ideally, height at the withers is 9 to 10 1/2 inches